D0117975

Adventures in
Coding

CALGARY PUBLIC LIBRARY

JUL   2016

Adventures in Coding

by Eva Holland and Chris Minnick

WILEY

Adventures in Coding

Published by
John Wiley & Sons, Inc.
10475 Crosspoint Boulevard
Indianapolis, IN 46256
www.wiley.com

Copyright © 2016 by John Wiley & Sons, Inc., Indianapolis, Indiana

Published simultaneously in Canada

ISBN: 978-1-119-23268-1
ISBN: 978-1-119-23269-8 (ebk)
ISBN: 978-1-119-23275-9 (ebk)

Manufactured in the United States of America

No part of this publication may be reproduced, stored in a retrieval system or transmitted in any form or by any means, electronic, mechanical, photocopying, recording, scanning or otherwise, except as permitted under Sections 107 or 108 of the 1976 United States Copyright Act, without either the prior written permission of the Publisher, or authorization through payment of the appropriate per-copy fee to the Copyright Clearance Center, 222 Rosewood Drive, Danvers, MA 01923, (978) 750-8400, fax (978) 646-8600. Requests to the Publisher for permission should be addressed to the Permissions Department, John Wiley & Sons, Inc., 111 River Street, Hoboken, NJ 07030, (201) 748-6011, fax (201) 748-6008, or online at http://www.wiley.com/go/permissions.

LIMIT OF LIABILITY/DISCLAIMER OF WARRANTY: THE PUBLISHER AND THE AUTHOR MAKE NO REPRESENTATIONS OR WARRANTIES WITH RESPECT TO THE ACCURACY OR COMPLETENESS OF THE CONTENTS OF THIS WORK AND SPECIFICALLY DISCLAIM ALL WARRANTIES, INCLUDING WITHOUT LIMITATION WARRANTIES OF FITNESS FOR A PARTICULAR PURPOSE. NO WARRANTY MAY BE CREATED OR EXTENDED BY SALES OR PROMOTIONAL MATERIALS. THE ADVICE AND STRATEGIES CONTAINED HEREIN MAY NOT BE SUITABLE FOR EVERY SITUATION. THIS WORK IS SOLD WITH THE UNDERSTANDING THAT THE PUBLISHER IS NOT ENGAGED IN RENDERING LEGAL, ACCOUNTING, OR OTHER PROFESSIONAL SERVICES. IF PROFESSIONAL ASSISTANCE IS REQUIRED, THE SERVICES OF A COMPETENT PROFESSIONAL PERSON SHOULD BE SOUGHT. NEITHER THE PUBLISHER NOR THE AUTHOR SHALL BE LIABLE FOR DAMAGES ARISING HEREFROM. THE FACT THAT AN ORGANIZATION OR WEB SITE IS REFERRED TO IN THIS WORK AS A CITATION AND/OR A POTENTIAL SOURCE OF FURTHER INFORMATION DOES NOT MEAN THAT THE AUTHOR OR THE PUBLISHER ENDORSES THE INFORMATION THE ORGANIZATION OR WEB SITE MAY PROVIDE OR RECOMMENDATIONS IT MAY MAKE. FURTHER, READERS SHOULD BE AWARE THAT INTERNET WEB SITES LISTED IN THIS WORK MAY HAVE CHANGED OR DISAPPEARED BETWEEN WHEN THIS WORK WAS WRITTEN AND WHEN IT IS READ.

For general information on our other products and services please contact our Customer Care Department within the United States at (877) 762-2974, outside the United States at (317) 572-3993 or fax (317) 572-4002.

Library of Congress Control Number: 2016931381

Trademarks: Wiley and the Wiley logo are trademarks or registered trademarks of John Wiley & Sons, Inc. and/or its affiliates, in the United States and other countries, and may not be used without written permission. All other trademarks are the property of their respective owners. John Wiley & Sons, Inc. is not associated with any product or vendor mentioned in this book.

This book is dedicated to the brave souls who have inspired in us a sense of adventure, especially David J. Holland, Patricia Minnick, Mary Ellen Holland, and Patrick Minnick.

Publisher's Acknowledgments

Some of the people who helped bring this book to market include the following:

Editorial

Series Creator: Carrie Anne Philbin

Professional Technology & Strategy Director: Barry Pruett

Acquisitions Editor: Aaron Black

Project Editor: Charlotte Kughen

Copy Editor: Kezia Endsley

Technical Editor: Mike Machado

Editorial Manager: Mary Beth Wakefield

Marketing

Marketing Manager: Lorna Mein

About the Authors

EVA HOLLAND is an accomplished author, trainer, and co-founder of WatzThis?, a company aimed at teaching technical topics in a fun and approachable manner. In addition to being co-author of this book, Eva is the co-author *JavaScript For Kids For Dummies* and *Coding with JavaScript For Dummies*. She enjoys tennis, music, reading, and the outdoors.

CHRIS MINNICK is a prolific published author, trainer, web developer, and co-founder of WatzThis?. Chris loves sharing his knowledge with others and has trained thousands of adults and kids in computer programming. As an author, his published books include *JavaScript For Kids For Dummies*, *Coding with JavaScript For Dummies*, *Beginning HTML5, CSS3 For Dummies*, and *Webkit For Dummies*. Chris is an avid reader, writer, swimmer, and musician.

Authors' Acknowledgments

This book is the result of a team effort, not only by your authors, but also by a talented crew of editors and other professionals who are credited on an earlier page.

Thank you to everyone at Wiley, including our Project Editor Charlotte Kughen, Acquisitions Editor Aaron Black, Copy Editor Kezia Endsley, Illustrator Sarah Wright, and Senior Editorial Assistant Cherie Case. A very special thank you to our Technical Editors Gavin Machado and Mike Machado. Thank you to Jay Silver for advising us in the initial stages of the book and for his role in the creation of Scratch.

Thank you also to our agent, Carole Jelen of Waterside Productions, as well as to our friends and families.

Contents

Adventure 2

Where in the World Is Scratch? 39

Adventure 3

Using Control Blocks 61

Adventure 4

Using Sensing Blocks 83

Adventure 5

Using Event Blocks 107

Adventure 6

Variables and Lists......................137

Adventure 7

Using Operators in Scratch............... 159

Introduction

ARE YOU A fearless adventurer? Do you like to set sail on new ventures and learn new skills? Do you want to learn how to use technology to turn your ideas into reality? Are you curious about computer programming, but aren't sure where to start? If your answer to these questions is a confident "yes!" then this book is for you!

Like people, computers can be talked to in a variety of languages. Computer programming, or *coding*, is a way for people to talk to computers. Many computer languages are similar to one another, so once you know one programming language, it's much easier to learn another one.

Adventures in Coding introduces you to the world of programming, using Scratch.

What Is Scratch?

Scratch is for anyone new to coding. It's a great place to begin your lifelong adventures in the world of computer programming. Scratch introduces programming concepts in a fun and approachable way. Using simple drag-and-drop features, you can create real computer programs while learning the fundamentals of coding.

Who Should Read This Book?

Adventures in Coding is a great starting point for any young person who is interested in learning how to create games, apps, and art on a computer.

What You Will Learn

Adventures in Coding introduces and guides you through the world of coding using Scratch. You learn the ins and outs of the Scratch universe—from learning about the features of the Project Editor, to connecting with fellow "Scratchers" and sharing projects.

Adventures in Coding teaches you how to create fun games, animate characters, build interactive projects, and more!

How This Book Is Structured

Each chapter of this book is an adventure of its own. With each adventure, you learn a new aspect of Scratch while building on what you already learned. Each adventure finishes with a completed project.

What You Need to Use This Book

The Scratch programming interface lives on the web. All you need to get started and complete the adventures in this book is a computer with a web browser (such as Chrome, Safari, Firefox, or Internet Explorer) and an Internet connection. No experience is expected or necessary. There is nothing you need to purchase or install. Scratch is always free, to anyone!

Conventions

Throughout the book, there are some special boxes to guide and support you. They use the following key:

 These boxes explain new concepts or terms.

 These boxes provide tips to make your life easier.

 These boxes include important things to watch out for.

These boxes further explain the inner workings of programs.

These boxes provide explanations or additional information about the topic at hand.

These boxes point you to videos on the companion website.

You will also find two sets of sidebars in the book. *Challenge* sidebars give you extra suggestions for expanding on the projects in the book. *Digging into the Code* sidebars further explain how some of the more complex programs work.

Companion Website

To download the videos mentioned in this book, visit the companion website at www.wiley.com/go/adventuresincoding.

Contact Us

Your authors, Chris and Eva, would love to hear about your progress in coding. You can reach out to us with questions, or to show us a cool project you've created, by visiting www.watzthis.com or emailing us at info@watzthis.com.

Adventure 1

Scratching the Surface

PROGRAMMING COMPUTERS IS a lot of fun. It's also a skill that many people see as mysterious and even magical. This chapter unmasks programming to show you just how easy it can be to start your own coding adventure.

Coding Is Everywhere

Computer programming, also known as **coding**, is how people tell computers what to do. What sorts of things can you do after you learn to program? For starters, you can write your own computer games, create modifications (or "mods") for existing games, program robots to do your bidding, create beautiful computer art and animations, and instruct your computer to play songs! The best part is that the whole time you're doing all these fun things, you're learning a valuable skill that is in sky-high demand!

Coding is a common name for computer programming. When you code, you're using a computer language to tell computers what to do.

Can you think of other things that computers can do? Think of all the things that programmers can tell computers to do. There are hundreds, or thousands, of things.

Think about all the things you see computers do every day—and not just the fun things. Computer programs are used to create new medicines, design buildings, do complex mathematics, control cars, and so much more.

This is the amazing world in which computer programmers live; we get to solve interesting problems every day and do things that other people see as magic.

Speaking the Language of Machines

All sorts of different people are programmers. Programmers come from different places and countries, with different experiences and different training. They speak different languages, have many different interests, and program for different reasons. What they have in common is that they've learned to speak at least one language that is understood by computers.

A **programmer** is a person who writes computer programs.

Computers don't speak the same languages that people do. People speak languages such as English, French, Spanish, Portuguese, Japanese, and many others. Computers speak machine language. Machine language is a difficult-to-read (for us) language that uses numbers to provide instructions to computers.

If machine language were the only way people could talk to computers, coding would be difficult. Fortunately, people have invented languages, called **programming languages**, which make it easier for people to talk to computers. Here are some examples of programming languages:

- JavaScript
- BASIC
- Perl
- PHP
- Python
- Java
- Visual Basic
- C

- C++

- Scratch

These languages all have one thing in common: They take words and symbols that people understand and translate them into words and symbols that computers understand.

A **programming language** is a language used for giving instructions to computers.

The examples in this book use Scratch. Scratch is a language that was invented at the Massachusetts Institute of Technology (MIT). It was designed to be easy for beginners to learn while using (and teaching) all of the most important things that programmers need to know.

Knowing Your Coding Lingo

You already know some of the lingo of coding. You know that "coding" is just another name for "computer programming," and you know that people who do computer programming—or coding—are called computer programmers (or coders).

Programming languages, like human languages, are made up of different parts. In English, we have nouns, verbs, adjectives, pronouns, and other parts of speech, not to mention punctuation, and they form sentences and paragraphs. In programming languages, you combine different statements (also known as **commands**) to make computer programs, which are also known as **applications** (or *apps*).

A **command** is an instruction, written in a programming language, that tells a computer to do a task.

An **application** is a set of programming commands that follow each other in a particular order to accomplish tasks. Application is another name for a computer program.

Scratch, and certain other programming languages, use the term **script**. Script is just another name for a program.

A **script** is another term for a computer program that is smaller and more limited than an application.

There are a lot of specialized words in coding that all have very specific meanings, and you'll find that sometimes there are many different words for the same thing. For this reason, we've included a glossary at the back of this book where you can look up or remind yourself of the meaning of terms you're not familiar with.

One of the greatest things about Scratch is that it's easy to dive right into! To get started, you don't need to learn a lot of new concepts or vocabulary. So enough talk! Let's begin!

Writing Your First Scratch Program

When we were growing up, kids didn't care about learning a specific style of dance. Instead of trying to learn complicated dance moves like the cha-cha or the hustle, we ran around like lunatics, jumping off of things, and we sometimes got hurt in the process. Your first Scratch program will be a simulator of an old-fashioned punk rock mosh pit.

Figure 1-1 shows what the finished product will look like. If you imagine the two characters in the figure bouncing off the walls and off each other while a drumbeat plays, you'll have a good idea of the program you'll be learning to make.

Joining Scratch

In order to create, save, and share your programs on the Scratch website, you need to use your favorite web browser to visit `http://scratch.mit.edu`, where you can sign up for a free account. When you go to the website, you see a screen that looks similar to Figure 1-2.

FIGURE 1-1 Your first Scratch program

Join Scratch link

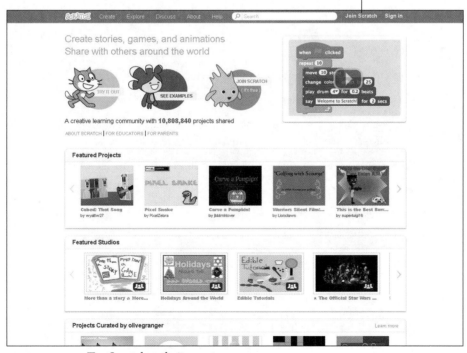

FIGURE 1-2 The Scratch website

Follow these steps to create your free account:

1. Click the Join Scratch link in the upper-right corner or center of the screen.

   The Join Scratch window opens.

2. Type a username into the field labeled Choose a Scratch Username.

Your username is how Scratch will know you and how other users will see you when you start to share programs. Be creative! Choosing a username can be fun! For everyone's safety, a good username shouldn't reveal any personal information, such as your full name, age, gender, or address. Try personalizing your username by including the name of your favorite sports team or musical group.

3. Choose a password and enter it into the Password and Confirm Password fields.

When creating your password, avoid using information that other people are likely to know, such as your address or birthday. Your password should be something you can remember, but it should also contain numbers or punctuation to make it more secure.

4. Click Next.

   You see the second screen of the signup form.

5. Enter your birthday, gender, and country and then click Next.

6. When you're asked for an email address, enter your email address in both the Email Address and Confirm Email Address fields and click Next.

   Scratch sends a confirmation email to the address you provided.

7. Click the OK Let's Go! button.

8. Check your email. When you get the email from Scratch, click the link in it to confirm your account.

Now you're ready to go. The next section tells you how to start coding!

Meeting Scratch the Cat

After you've joined Scratch and you're ready to start coding, click the Create tab in the top menu of the screen. When the new page loads, you see the scratch Project Editor, which looks like Figure 1-3.

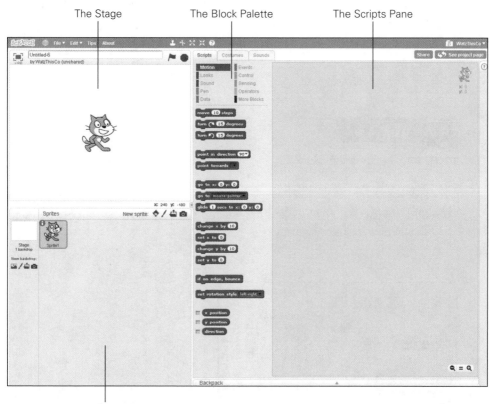

FIGURE 1-3 The Scratch Project Editor

Don't worry too much about what the things on this screen do. We'll be talking in detail about each part later. For now, let's build something!

See that cool cat in the middle of the screen? Her name is Scratch the Cat. Every new Scratch program starts with her sitting right there, waiting for instructions from you. The area where she lives is called the Stage. This is where all the action of your program takes place.

Below the Stage is an area called the Sprite Pane. The Sprite Pane shows small images of each of the characters (also known as sprites) in your program.

To the right of the Stage is a rectangle containing differently shaped blocks. This is called the Block Palette. Think of it like a painter's palette, where a painter selects the colors that she wants to paint with before combining those colors to make a painting on a canvas.

To the right of Block Palette is the Scripts Area. This is your canvas, where you put together the blocks selected from the Block Palette to make your sprites do things.

Moving Scratch Around

To get a better idea of how all the pieces fit together, follow these steps to make Scratch the Cat do something:

1. Find the block that says move 10 steps. This is the move () block. It looks like Figure 1-4.

FIGURE 1-4 The move block

2. Click the move () block and drag it into the Scripts Area. Your Scripts Area should now look like Figure 1-5.

FIGURE 1-5 The Scripts Area, with one block

3. Double-click the move ( ) block and watch what Scratch the Cat does. Did you see it? She moved slightly to the right.

4. Click the number 10 inside the move block to highlight it and change the 10 to 20.

5. Double-click the block. Now Scratch moves twice as far as she did before.

6. Try changing the value in the move ( ) block to an even larger number and see what happens.

Connecting Blocks

Notice that the move block looks a bit like a puzzle piece. It works a bit like a puzzle piece too! Any time you see a block shaped like this, you know that you can attach it to another block.

Follow these steps to put some blocks together to make Scratch the Cat do something more complicated:

1. Find the turn clockwise block in the Block Palette. Figure 1-6 shows what the block looks like.

   Notice that it has the same shape as the move block.

FIGURE 1-6 The turn clockwise block

2. Drag the turn clockwise block to the Stage and snap it to the bottom of the move block. When the blocks are connected, they look as shown in Figure 1-7.

FIGURE 1-7 Your first connected blocks

Double-click the combination of blocks and watch what happens on the Stage. The instructions on the first block happen, and then the instructions on the second block happen!

By right-clicking the combination of blocks and selecting Duplicate, from the menu you can create an exact copy of the block combination. Try it out! Then snap the two combinations of blocks together so that they look like Figure 1-8.

FIGURE 1-8 Duplicating blocks

Now click the whole thing and watch what Scratch the Cat does.

Looping Movements

If you want to make Scratch the Cat do this turning and moving thing over and over, you could keep making as many duplicates as you want of these same blocks, or you could create what's called a loop.

A **loop** is a block that causes the commands contained within it to repeat one or more times.

Use the following steps to create a loop:

1. Separate the second two blocks from the first two by clicking the second move block and dragging downward.

2. Right-click the second set of blocks and then select Delete from the context menu to remove the block set from the Stage.

3. Click the word Control in the color-coded menu in the Block Palette. Then find the forever block (see Figure 1-9) inside the Control Block Palette.

FIGURE 1-9 The `forever` block

4. Drag the `forever` block to the Stage and place it over the `move` and `turn` blocks so that it snaps around them, as shown in Figure 1-10.

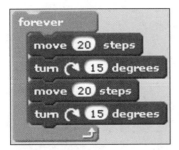

FIGURE 1-10 Wrapping the `forever` block around other blocks

When snapping blocks together and inside of each other, be sure they're completely fitted into place and are not overlapping; otherwise, your script will not run.

5. Double-click the combination of blocks and watch what happens!

Scratch the Cat keeps moving and turning forever . . . or until you click the red Stop Sign shown in Figure 1-11.

FIGURE 1-11 The Stop Sign

6. Click the Stop Sign to end the loop.

There are other ways to stop a loop. You learn all those tricks in Adventure 3, "Using Control Blocks"!

Starting at the Green Flag

Next to the Stop Sign, you see a Green Flag. This is also known as the Run button. You can press it to start all the action in a program, rather than double-clicking on the blocks.

To enable the Green Flag for your program, follow these steps:

1. In the Block Palette, click Events, as shown in Figure 1-12.

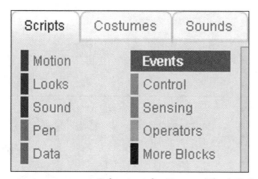

FIGURE 1-12 Selecting the Events Block Palette

Remember that in Scratch, a **script** is a series of connected commands that cause a sprite to do some task.

2. Drag the when green flag clicked block to the Scripts Area and snap it onto the top of your existing script. Your script should now look like Figure 1-13.

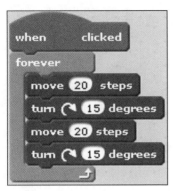

FIGURE 1-13 Adding the Green Flag event to your program

3. Click the Green Flag above the Stage to see your program run.

Scratch the Cat starts running in circles.

4. When you're done watching Scratch the Cat run in circles, click the Stop Sign.

Bouncing Off the Walls

Moving in circles is cool, but it's time to add some new instructions so Scratch can roam a bit more. Use the following steps to tell Scratch to do more things:

1. Click the `turn clockwise` block and drag it out of the Scripts Area and back into the Block Palette. It disappears from your script, which now looks like Figure 1-14.

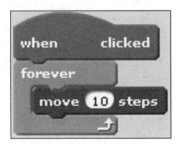

FIGURE 1-14 The program after you've removed the `turn clockwise` block

2. Click the Green Flag to run the program.

Scratch runs right off the screen and keeps on running forever!

3. Click the Stop Sign.

4. Click Motion in the Block Palette and drag the `if on edge, bounce` block to the Stage. Snap it underneath the `move` block, as shown in Figure 1-15.

FIGURE 1-15 Adding an `if on edge, bounce` block

5. Click the Green Flag to see what Scratch does now.

   She runs around, bouncing off the walls, until you click the Stop Sign.

That's more like it! You're getting closer to having a mosh pit, but it's not really a proper mosh pit unless there are other dancers. In the next section, you add a second character to the dance floor.

Creating a Sprite

Look for the Sprite Pane at the bottom of the screen. At the top of it, you see New Sprite: and then some icons. Scratch has numerous built-in characters besides Scratch the Cat that you can use in your programs. You can also create your own characters by uploading a graphic or even by taking a picture!

1. Click the Choose Sprite from Library icon, which is the first icon to the right of New Sprite.

2. Browse through the Sprite Library and find a sprite you like.

3. When you find the sprite you want to use, click it, and then click the OK button at the bottom of the Sprite Library.

   Your new sprite is added to the Stage and to the Sprite Pane.

After you add your second sprite, you see that the Scripts Area becomes blank. That's because each sprite has its own Scripts Area that is visible when that sprite is selected. Because you just added this sprite, it doesn't yet have any scripts tied to it.

Press the Green Flag. You see that your first sprite bounces around the screen while your new one just sits there.

To animate your new sprite, follow these steps:

1. In the Sprite Pane, click Scratch the Cat.

   You should now see her script appear in the Scripts Pane.

2. Click the first block in the Scripts Area (the when green flag clicked block) and drag it to the Sprite Pane, dropping it on top of your new sprite.

3. Click on your second sprite in the Sprite Pane.

   You see that the scripts from the first sprite have been copied over to the new sprite!

4. Click the Green Flag.

   Now, both characters are bouncing around like maniacs. Fun!

Handling Collisions on the Dance Floor

You may have noticed a strange thing about how your two sprites interact. In real dancing, when two people bump into each other, a collision happens and they bounce away from each other. It's time to make these sprites collide and bounce!

Select one of your sprites in the Sprite Pane. Because they have the same script now, it doesn't matter which sprite you choose. You're going to add the collision script to one of the sprites and then copy it to the other.

1. Click the Control Block Palette to open it.

2. Look for the if ... then block. It looks like Figure 1-16.

FIGURE 1-16 The if ... then block

3. Drag the if ... then block to the Stage so that it's snapped to the bottom of the if on edge, bounce block, as shown in Figure 1-17.

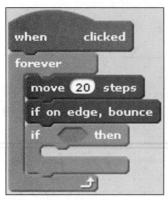

FIGURE 1-17 Adding an `if ... then` block to the script

Next, you're going to use a new type of block—a Sensing block—to detect whether the sprites are touching.

1. Click the Sensing Block Palette.

2. Drag the `touching ()` block into the hexagon-shaped empty spot in the `if ... then` block.

   The empty spot expands to fit the `touching` block, and the new block snaps into place, as shown in Figure 1-18.

   Notice that the `touching ()` block has a drop-down menu inside of it.

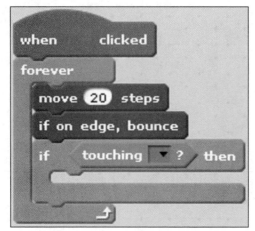

FIGURE 1-18 Adding a Sensing block to the `if ... then` block

3. Click the drop-down menu inside the `touching ()` block and select the name of the other character on the Stage.

   Now, whenever this sprite is touching the other sprite, it does the actions inside of the `if ... then` block.

4. Click the Motion Block Palette to open it.

5. Drag the `turn clockwise` block from the Motion Block Palette and snap it inside of the `if ... then` block.

6. Drag the `move` block to the Scripts Area and snap it to the bottom of the `turn clockwise` block.

7. Change the value in the `turn clockwise` block to 20 degrees.

8. Change the value in the `move` block to 30 steps.

   Your program now looks like Figure 1-19.

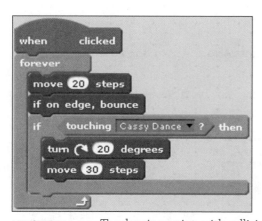

FIGURE 1-19 The dancing script, with collisions programmed

9. Copy the script to the other sprite by dragging it and dropping it onto the thumbnail image of the other sprite in the Sprite Pane.

10. Click the other sprite in the Sprite Pane.

    You see both the old script (without the `if ... then` block) and the new one. If it looks like there's only one script, click and drag on the script to find the other script hiding behind it.

11. Right-click the old script and choose Delete from the context menu to remove the old script.

12. Finally, change the value in the drop-down menu inside the `touching` block to the name of the other sprite, so that each sprite turns and moves when they bump into the other sprite.

13. Click the Green Flag to start the crazy dancing!

Slowing It Down

This dancing is way too fast. If this keeps up, the city council is for sure going to pass a law banning dancing! Follow these steps to slow down the dancing.

1. Go to the Control Block Palette and find the `wait` block. It looks like Figure 1-20.

FIGURE 1-20 The `wait` block

2. Drag the `wait` block into the Scripts Area and snap it in above the first `move` block.

The `wait` block should now be the first block inside the `forever` block, as shown in Figure 1-21.

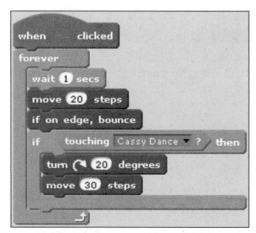

FIGURE 1-21 Adding the `wait` block to the script

The `wait` block does just as it says: It causes the sprite to wait a certain number of seconds (or a fraction of a second) before performing the next command.

If you only want to slow down the dancing, not bring it to a stop, you can change the value in the `wait` block to a very small amount of time.

3. Click the oval inside the `wait` block to highlight the number and change it to 0.1.

4. Click the Green Flag to see that one of the sprites is now moving much more slowly than the other.

5. Apply the same wait change to the other sprite.

Congratulations! You've built your first computer program! In the next part of this adventure, we take you on a tour of the Scratch Project Editor. You're already somewhat familiar with it from building the Mosh Pit Simulator, but read on, because the next few pages tell you the lingo and the ins and outs of Scratch that you need to know in order to build exciting projects.

Learning the Scratch Environment

Beginning with version 2.0, the Scratch Project Editor is available as an online application as well as an offline application. What this means is that you can download Scratch to your computer and install it, or you can program with Scratch through the website at `http://scratch.mit.edu`.

The benefit of using the offline version is that you don't need an Internet connection. Also, the online version sometimes has slowdowns and hiccups when a lot of people are using it at the same time. The offline version is immune to these problems.

In this book, we work with the online version. As you'll find out, the online version of Scratch has a ton of fun collaborative and sharing features that the offline version doesn't. Programming online makes it possible for you to share your work with your friends and to make new friends who can help you become a better coder.

If you want to install the offline version, check out the instructions in Appendix A (way in the back of the book). To complete most of the adventures in this book, both the offline or online versions of Scratch work great, and both are completely free to use.

Now that you understand the differences between the two versions of Scratch, let's start finding out how they work!

Exploring the Scratch Project Editor

Whether you go to `http://scratch.mit.edu` and click Create in the top menu bar or whether you're using the offline editor, the place where you do all your coding in Scratch is called the Scratch Project Editor.

The Scratch Project Editor is split into different sections. When you first open it, there are two sections on the left, one long one in the middle, and one on the right. We call these panes. You can think of them as being like panes of glass in a window. Unlike window panes, however, you can easily change the size of some of these panes.

TIPS & TRICKS

When you see a small arrow on the frame between two panes, you can click that arrow to change the size of a pane.

Notice that there's an arrow between the long skinny pane (which is called the Block Palette) and the two panes on the left (the Stage and the Sprite Pane). Click that arrow now. The pane on the right, the Scripts Area, becomes larger while the panes on the left get smaller, as shown in Figure 1-22.

This resizing feature is handy to know about when you're working with large scripts or blocks with complicated instructions because it lets you see more of your script at one time.

VIDEO

For a video that walks you through the Project Editor, visit the companion website at `www.wiley.com/go/adventuresincoding` and choose the Adventure 1 video.

The Toolbar

At the very top of the Scratch Project Editor is the toolbar. The toolbar gives you features that are useful for working with Scratch. Figure 1-23 shows what the toolbar looks like.

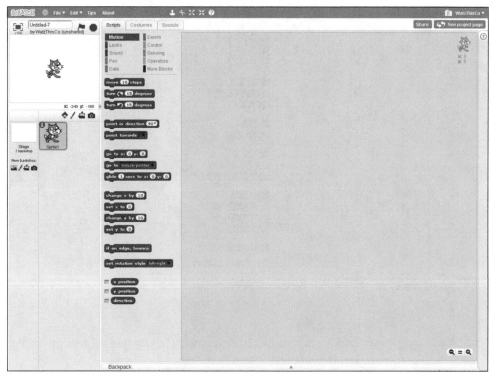

FIGURE 1-22 The Scratch Project Editor with adjusted panes

FIGURE 1-23 The Scratch Toolbar

The first link on the toolbar is the Scratch logo. Any time you click this logo, you're taken to the Scratch homepage. The Scratch homepage is where you can find out the latest happenings with other "Scratchers" whom you follow, where you can read the latest news about Scratch, view featured projects, and see lots of projects created by people all over the world. We recommend that you spend some time just exploring what sorts of things other people are creating with Scratch. There really are some amazing projects that people have created using Scratch.

To the right of the Scratch logo is the globe icon. Click this icon now to see a list of languages that Scratch works with. Scroll through this list. Pretty amazing, right? Try selecting one of these languages and watch how the Scratch Project Editor changes. Figure 1-24 shows the French version of Scratch.

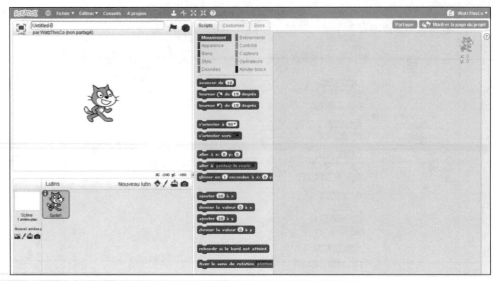

FIGURE 1-24 The French version of Scratch

If you want to get back to the English language version, just select English from the Language menu. (English is the first option in the menu.)

To the right of the Language menu is the File menu, as shown in Figure 1-25.

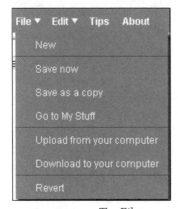

FIGURE 1-25 The File menu

The File menu contains links to create a new project, to save your current project, to go to your list of saved projects (called My Stuff), to upload projects from the offline version, and to revert to (or "go back to") a previously saved version of your project.

Next to the File menu is the Edit menu. The first item in the Edit menu is very important when you need it. It's the Undelete link. When there's nothing that's been recently deleted, the Undelete link is gray, indicating that there's nothing you can undelete. But, if you accidentally delete a script or a sprite, remember that Scratch has this feature, and that you can always come up to the Edit menu to undo your mistake.

To test out the Undelete link, follow these steps.

1. Right-click one of the sprites on the Stage and select Delete from the context menu, as shown in Figure 1-26.

   Oh no! You weren't supposed to delete that one! What a terrible mistake! But wait, there's an undelete option!

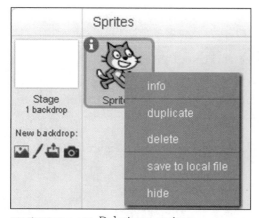

FIGURE 1-26 Deleting a sprite

2. Click the Edit menu in the toolbar. When it opens, you see that the Undelete link is now white, indicating that you can use it. Click the Undelete link now.

   Your sprite—and all the scripts associated with it—magically returns. Phew! That was a close one.

The next option on the Edit menu is the Small Stage Layout option. If you click this, you see that the Scripts Area gets larger, and the left panes get smaller; exactly like when you click the arrow to the right of the Stage.

The final option under the Edit menu is Turbo Mode. Turbo Mode causes scripts to run as fast as your computer can run them. This can be helpful for complex scripts that do a lot of drawing or animations.

The link next to the Edit menu is Tips. Click Tips now to see a menu come from the right side of the screen. Each of the items on the Tips menu is a tutorial that shows you how to do something different in Scratch.

The final link in the toolbar is About. It takes you to a page containing information about Scratch and the people who make and use it.

If you stay in the toolbar and look a little bit to the right, you see a list of icons that look like Figure 1-27. These icons give you access to some really handy features of Scratch.

FIGURE 1-27 The toolbar icons

The first is the Duplicate icon, which looks like Figure 1-28.

FIGURE 1-28 The Duplicate icon

To use duplicate, follow these steps:

1. Click the Duplicate icon. Your cursor turns into what looks like a rubber stamp.

2. Use the rubber stamp to click a script or a sprite in your program.

   An exact copy of the object you clicked will be created! If you duplicate a sprite, the number 2 is added to the sprite's name so that you can tell it from the original.

Next to the Duplicate icon is the Delete icon. To use the Delete icon, follow these steps:

1. Click the Delete icon (it looks like a pair of scissors) in the toolbar.

2. Use the scissors to click something on the Stage, in the Sprite Pane, or in the Scripts Area. Whatever you click is deleted.

Remember: You can get back something after you delete it by using the Undelete link under the Edit menu.

The next two icons on the toolbar are the Grow and Shrink tools. You can use these to make objects on the Stage larger or smaller. Try them out now to change the sizes of the sprites, as shown in Figure 1-29.

FIGURE 1-29 Sprites can be different sizes

Try running your Mosh Pit Simulator program with the sizes changed and notice how it affects the program and how big sprites run into the edges of the Stage and into other sprites more often.

The last item in the toolbar icons area is the Block Help tool. The Block Help tool gives you a quick review of how a block works. To use it, click the tool (it looks like a circle with a question mark in it) and then click a block on the screen. A help box opens on the right to give you more information about what you just clicked.

Next take a look at the right side of the toolbar. You see an icon that looks like a file folder with an S on it. This is a link to your My Stuff area. My Stuff is where all your saved projects are kept.

To the right of the My Stuff link is your username. Notice that it has an arrow pointing downward. If you click your username, a menu opens that contains links to your Profile, another link to My Stuff, an Account Setting link, and a Sign Out link.

The Profile page is where you can edit what other Scratch users see about you, including your picture, a little bit about yourself, a description of what you're working on (you might, for example, say "I'm reading *Adventures in Coding!*") and any shared and "favorited" projects that you have.

Our Profile page is shown in Figure 1-30.

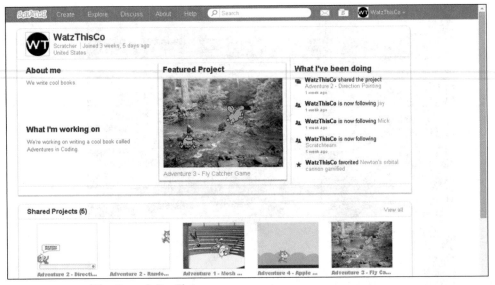

FIGURE 1-30 The Scratch Profile page

 It's fun to personalize your online profile. For your safety, don't include personal details such as your home address, phone number, or age.

That's it for the toolbar. The next section describes the Stage of the Scratch Project Editor.

The Stage

The Stage, as you've already learned, is where sprites act out the scripts that you write. At the top of the Stage are the Green Flag and the Stop Sign, which control whether a project is running or stopped.

To the left of the Green Flag and the Stop Sign is the Project Name area. This is a text input area where you can give your project any name that you like. For example, you might call the Mosh Pit simulator "Adventure 1 - Mosh Pit Simulator," as shown in Figure 1-31.

FIGURE 1-31 Give your project a name

The Stage Coordinates

Look at the bottom-right corner of the Stage. You see an *x* with a number after it and a *y* with a number after it. Click inside the Stage and then move your mouse around within it. Notice how the numbers next to *x* and *y* change as you move your mouse.

These numbers represent the position of your mouse in the Stage. Adventure 2, "Where in the World Is Scratch?," talks much more about these numbers.

The Backdrop Pane

In the lower-left corner of the Scratch Project Editor is the Backdrop Pane, which enables you to change the appearance of the Stage (called its backdrop) and add scripts to the Stage.

The Backdrop Pane looks like Figure 1-32.

FIGURE 1-32 The Backdrop Pane

When you start a new Scratch project, it has a white backdrop. You can change the backdrop of your project by using the New Backdrop menu. The New Backdrop menu looks like Figure 1-33.

FIGURE 1-33 New Backdrop menu

Click the first icon in the New Backdrop menu. The Backdrop Library opens in a window. Select one of the backdrops from the library and click OK. The backdrop is applied to your project.

Using the other backdrop icons, you can create a new backdrop by drawing it, uploading it, or taking a picture.

The Sprite Pane

The Sprite Pane is the area just below the Stage. It holds small images of each character, or sprite, in your program.

At the top of the Sprite Pane are the options for creating new sprites. These options are shown using four icons, as shown in Figure 1-34.

FIGURE 1-34 New sprite icons

Besides duplicating existing sprites, you can also create new sprites using any of the following methods:

- **Select them from the library.** The Scratch Library contains hundreds of different pictures and icons that you can use in any of your programs.

- **Paint the sprite.** When you click the Paint Brush tool in the New Sprite menu, the Paint Editor opens up, where you can draw your own sprite.

- **Upload a file.** If you have a picture or graphic that you want to use as a sprite, you can upload it here.

- **Take a picture.** If you have a camera on your computer, you can use it to take a picture and use that photo as a sprite!

The Sprite Info Pane

When you select a sprite in the Sprite Pane, it gets a blue border around it and an *i* icon in the upper-left corner, as shown in Figure 1-35.

FIGURE 1-35 A selected sprite

Click the *i* icon for one of your sprites to see the Sprite Info Pane. You can use the Sprite Info Pane to find out or change several settings related to a sprite, including

- The sprite's name

- The sprite's current location

- The sprite's rotation

- Whether or not the sprite can be rotated, or just flipped left and right

- Whether users can drag the sprite in the Stage

- Whether the sprite is visible or hidden

The Scripts Area

The Scripts Area is where you assemble blocks associated with a sprite into scripts. You can have as many blocks in your sprite's Scripts Area as you want. However, for large programs, a sprite's Scripts Area can get pretty crowded, as shown in Figure 1-36.

Within the middle area of the interface, there are three tabs: Scripts, Costume, and Sounds. Clicking any of these labels determines which of these three palettes are active.

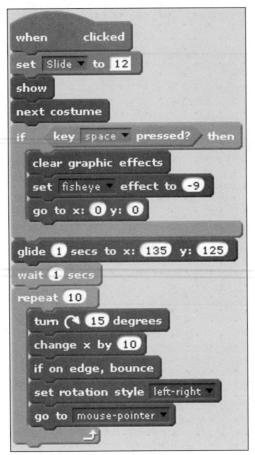

FIGURE 1-36 The Scripts Area can get pretty crowded. In Adventure 9, you find out how to reduce or eliminate block clutter by creating your very own custom blocks.

The Block Palette

You access the Block Palette when you select the Scripts tab. This is where you can select blocks and drag them into the Scripts Area. Scratch contains 10 different categories of blocks, which you can select by clicking the words in the menu of the Block Palette. These 10 categories are

- Motion
- Looks
- Sound
- Pen

- Data

- Events

- Control

- Sensing

- Operators

- More Blocks

The Costume Pane

Next to the Scripts tab is the Costumes tab. This opens the Costumes Pane, as shown in Figure 1-37.

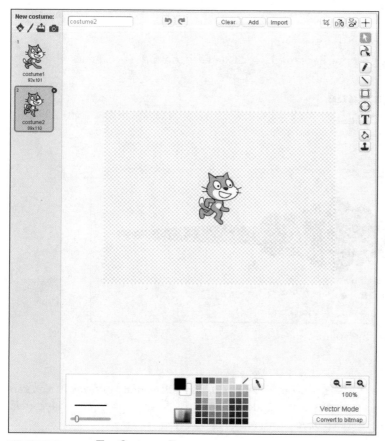

FIGURE 1-37 The Costume Pane

Costumes are alternate looks for a sprite. Any sprite may have just a single costume, or it may have multiple costumes. The default Scratch the Cat sprite has two costumes, as shown in Figure 1-38. When you switch between these two costumes, Scratch appears to be walking.

FIGURE 1-38 Scratch's two costumes

You can use the Costume Pane to view, edit, and delete a sprite's costumes.

The Sound Pane

If you click the Sounds tab, the Sound Pane opens, as shown in Figure 1-39.

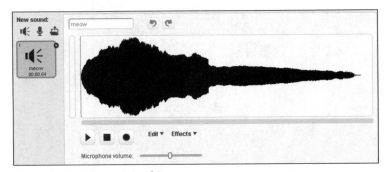

FIGURE 1-39 The Sound Pane

The Sound Pane is where you can create, load, and edit sounds in Scratch. You can record your own sounds, upload sounds from files, or download and use prerecorded sounds that other Scratch users have created.

Working with Colors and Shapes in Scratch

By now, you've probably noticed that the blocks in Scratch are color-coded according to their function. For example, Motion blocks are blue, Data blocks are orange, and Operator blocks are green.

Blocks are also shape-coded according to their function. Pay particular attention to the shapes of blocks as you gain more knowledge of Scratch. Not only do they indicate how blocks fit together, but they also tell you how you can expect the blocks to interact inside of your projects.

The blocks in Scratch have the following shapes:

- **Stack Block.** These are rectangular blocks that look like puzzle pieces. They can fit above or below other blocks. They represent actions that do something in your program. The `move` block is an example of a **stack block**.

- **Cap Block.** A cap block looks like a puzzle piece that belongs on the edge. Cap blocks are used to stop a script or project. The `stop` block is an example of a **cap block**.

- **Reporter Block.** These are the oval blocks that contain a value. They stand for a number or piece of text and are designed to fit inside of other blocks that require a value. An example of a **reporter block** is the `size` block.

- **Hat Block.** These blocks have curved tops that look like hats. These are blocks that can trigger the start of a linked together series of blocks. An example of this type of block is the `when green flag clicked` block.

- **C-Block.** These blocks are shaped like a "C." They have a space that looks like a mouth, so that other blocks can fit inside of them. The C-block performs loops or makes decisions. The `forever` block is an example of a **C-block**.

- **Boolean Block.** These blocks are hexagonal, with points on both sides. When used in a program, they stand for a value that's either true or false. The `touching ()` block is an example of a **Boolean block**.

Further Adventures in Coding

There's another important thing that we need to tell you about before we move on to the next adventure: That's the Scratch website at `https://scratch.mit.edu/`.

The Scratch website is a great place to get ideas for new projects, to learn more about Scratch, and to share what you're working on with other Scratch users (called "Scratchers").

On the homepage you'll see a menu at the top. Click on the Explore tab. From there, you can view and explore some of the many projects that people just like you have created using Scratch. You can also view different studios. A studio is a place where people can display projects, like an art gallery. And just like an art gallery, Scratch Studios have **curators**.

DEFINITIONS

A **curator** is a manager or guardian in charge of the selections displayed in an art museum. Some Scratch Studios allow you to become curators when you follow them; other studios require you to be invited to become a curator.

You can create your very own studio from your profile by clicking My Stuff. You can also apply to be a Scratch homepage curator! This means that you would be in charge of selecting your favorite projects to be displayed on the front page of the Scratch website. Visit `https://scratch.mit.edu/studios/386359/projects/` to apply.

There are tons of features and interesting things to discover. Before you move on to Adventure 2, take some time to visit `http://scratch.mit.edu`.

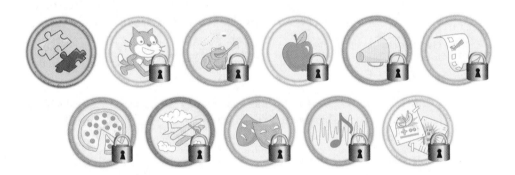

Achievement Unlocked: **Your First Scratch Project**

In the Next Adventure

In the next adventure, you dive further into the Scratch Project Editor and learn about all the different ways that sprites can move around the Stage!

Adventure 2

Where in the World Is Scratch?

IN THIS ADVENTURE, you find out how distance is measured in Scratch. You also learn the different ways to move sprites around the Stage, and how to rotate and even spin sprites. You discover how to customize the backdrop so that action in your program can look like it's taking place in a location of your choosing or creation—even in your own home or backyard!

Setting the Stage

Take a look at the Stage in Scratch. It's a relatively small part of the Project Editor, but this is where every visible part of your program will happen. The amount of space that it takes up on your screen depends on how large your computer monitor is. On most screens, it takes up about a quarter, or maybe less, of the screen, as shown in Figure 2-1.

In spite of its relatively small size, the Stage is made up of 172,800 tiny dots. Each of these tiny dots is called a **pixel**.

A **pixel** is one of many tiny dots that make up an image on a computer screen.

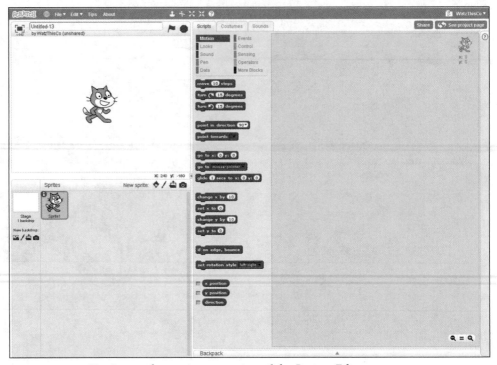

FIGURE 2-1 The Stage takes up just a portion of the Project Editor

If you use the Small Stage Layout, as shown in Figure 2-2, there are still 172,800 different pixels on the Stage. You may be wondering how this can be true, when the Stage is clearly much smaller in the Small Stage Layout. The answer is that the Small Stage Layout pushes all the pixels on the stage closer to each other, making each pixel closer to its neighbor and making all the sprites on the Stage smaller. So, when you move Scratch the Cat by ten steps in the normal, full-size Stage, she looks like she moves farther than she does in the Small Stage Layout, as shown in Figure 2-3. This is because the pixels are spread farther apart in the Full-Size Stage Layout than they are in the Small Stage Layout.

You can change to the Small Stage Layout by clicking the arrow between the Block Palette and the Stage, or by selecting Small Stage Layout from the Edit menu.

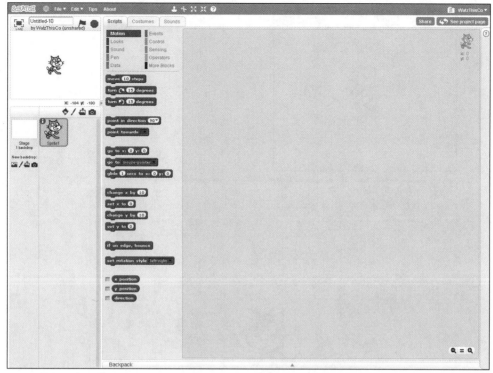

FIGURE 2-2 The Small Stage Layout

Interacting with the Stage

When a program isn't running, you can drag sprites around the Stage. Follow these steps to try this out yourself:

1. From the Scratch homepage, click the Create tab to make a new Scratch project.

   The Project Editor opens with a single sprite, Scratch the Cat, on the Stage.

2. Click and drag Scratch the Cat to another location on the Stage.

3. Try dragging Scratch the Cat as far off the Stage to the right as you can.

   Notice that she snaps back to where you started dragging her.

4. Now, try dragging Scratch just a little bit off the Stage.

   Notice that she stays in the new position, with part of her on the Stage and part offstage.

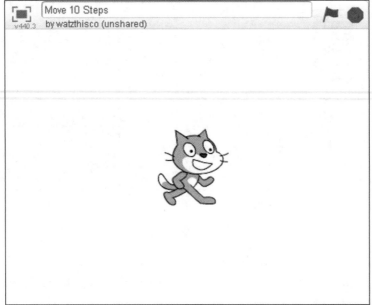

FIGURE 2-3 The Small Stage Layout (on top) has the same number of pixels as the full-size Stage (on bottom), but the pixels are closer together.

For now, leave Scratch the Cat where she is. The next section moves into exploring the backdrop; later you'll come back to learning about the different ways you can move Scratch the Cat around the Stage.

Customizing the Backdrop

The backdrop is a special sprite that covers the entire background of the Stage. You can think of it as the backdrop in a photo studio or the backdrop on a theater stage.

As with a theater's stage backdrop, you can change the scene and mood of a Scratch program by switching the backdrop. In the previous adventure, you chose a new backdrop from the library. In this adventure, you find out how to draw your own backdrop and to create one from a picture!

To create your own custom backdrop, click the Paint Brush icon from the New Backdrop menu, which is in the lower-left corner of the Project Editor. The Paint Editor opens, as shown in Figure 2-4.

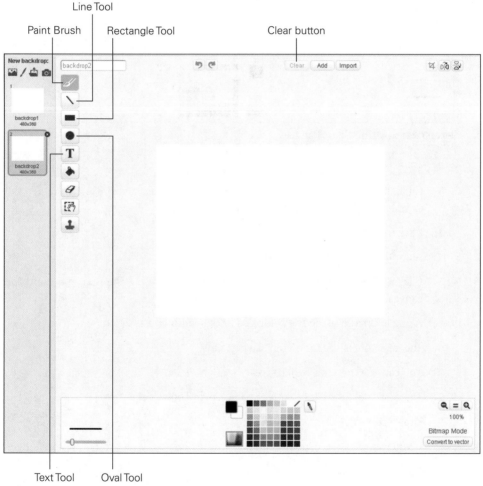

FIGURE 2-4 The Paint Editor

The Backdrop Pane appears to the left of the Paint Editor. It has small images (also known as thumbnails) of your project's backdrops. Currently, both thumbnails are blank (white), and backdrop2 should be the selected backdrop.

To the right of the Backdrop Pane is the Paint Editor Toolbox. Follow these steps to experiment with each of the tools:

1. Click the Paint Brush, which is the first tool in the toolbox. (Refer to Figure 2-4 for the location of the tools.)

2. Choose a color from the Color Palette at the bottom of the Paint Editor, as shown in Figure 2-5.

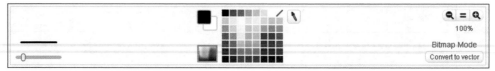

FIGURE 2-5 The Color Palette

3. Choose your Paint Brush thickness by moving the Brush Size Bar under the sample line to the left of the Color Palette.

4. Click inside the blank canvas.

   A dot of the color you selected is created.

5. Click and hold down the mouse button while you drag the mouse around the canvas.

   A line is created using the color and brush width you selected.

6. The next tool is the Line Tool. Click it now.

   You can use the Line Tool to create straight lines.

7. The next tool in the toolbar is the Rectangle Tool. Click it now.

8. Drag a rectangle on the canvas.

   If you want a perfect square, hold down the Shift key while you draw a rectangle.

9. Click the Oval Tool.

   It works the same as the Rectangle Tool! Hold the Shift key to make a perfect circle.

10. Click the Clear button at the top of the canvas to erase everything in the canvas.

11. Try drawing a scene (perhaps with trees, houses, and animals) on the canvas using the Paint Brush, the Rectangle Tool, and the Oval Tool. The scene that we drew is shown in Figure 2-6.

FIGURE 2-6 A lovely scene created in the Paint Editor

Next on the Paint Editor Toolbox is the Text Tool. With the Text Tool, you can type words, in any color, and with a variety of different **fonts**.

Fonts are also known as typefaces. They are the design of a complete set of letters and numbers. For example, if you look closely, you'll notice that the letters used in this definition look different from the letters used in the rest of the text of the book. That is because the letters in this definition box use a different font.

Here's how to use the Text Tool:

1. Click the letter *T* in the Paint Editor Toolbar. (Refer to Figure 2-4 for the location of the Text Tool.)

2. Click anywhere in the canvas to the right of the toolbar.

3. Type something, such as your name.

   You see the letters appear on the canvas.

4. In the pane at the bottom of the Paint Editor, select a different font from the Font menu.

   Notice that the text you typed changes to the new font.

5. Select a different color for your text by clicking a color in the Color Palette.

Using a Picture Backdrop

If you have a camera attached to your computer, or if you have pictures stored on your computer, you can use one of these as a backdrop. To upload your own picture to use as your backdrop, follow these instructions:

1. Under New Backdrop, click the icon that looks like a file folder with an arrow coming out of it.

   A file picker dialog box opens.

2. Browse to a picture on your computer and select it.

 Pictures that are wider than they are tall work best for backdrops. If you use your phone to take a picture to use as a backdrop in Scratch, hold your phone the long way in order to take a landscape picture.

3. Click the Open button to import the picture as a new backdrop, as shown in Figure 2-7.

Taking a Picture of the Stage

There's one more thing that you can do with the Stage. You can take a picture of it! To take a picture of the Stage, right-click (or click the Stage while holding down the Ctrl key). A menu opens that contains a single option: Save Picture of Stage.

Click Save Picture of Stage to open a File Save dialog box. You can use this to save an image file to your computer. After you've saved an image file, you can send it to a friend, share it on Facebook, or even print it out!

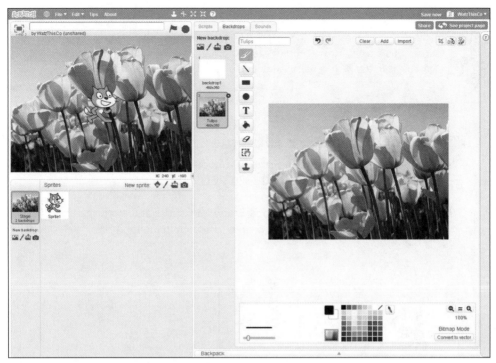

FIGURE 2-7 Creating a custom background from a photo

Understanding Coordinates on the Stage

As mentioned previously, the Stage is made up of 172,800 pixels. But, how do we know that without counting each one?

We know because the Stage has a width of 480 pixels and a height of 360 pixels. If you multiply 480 by 360, you get 172,800.

In Scratch, you can put sprites anywhere on the Stage (and even off the Stage) by telling the sprite to go to a certain vertical (up and down) position and a certain horizontal (left and right) position. Each pixel that you move a sprite is known in Scratch as a step. So, when you make Scratch the Cat move ten steps, you're really making her move ten pixels.

Horizontal positions are represented by the letter x and vertical positions are represented by the letter y.

Scientists, programmers, and mapmakers call the system of using *x* and *y* to tell where you are a Cartesian coordinate system. This system was invented by René Descartes in the 17th century, and people have been using it ever since!

Taking Center Stage

When you make a new sprite in Scratch, it appears in the center of the Stage. The center of the Stage has an *x* value of 0 and a *y* value of 0.

You can open the Sprite Info Pane for a brand new sprite and see just to the right of the sprite's thumbnail that it's at the center, as shown in Figure 2-8.

FIGURE 2-8 Sprites start out at center stage

If you move a sprite away from the center of the Stage, you can return it to the center (or anywhere else) by using the go to x: () and y: () block. To try out this block, follow these steps:

1. Click and drag a sprite away from the center, toward the upper-right corner of the Stage.

2. Find the go to x: () and y: () block in the Motion Block Palette and drag it to the Scripts Area, as shown in Figure 2-9.

FIGURE 2-9 Dragging the go to x: () and y: () block to the Scripts Area

3. Click in the oval next to x: and change the number to 0.

4. Click in the oval next to y: and change the number to 0.

5. Double-click the `go to x: () and y: ()` block.

The sprite jumps back to the center of the Stage!

Moving Left, Right, Up, and Down

With four simple rules, you can figure out how to move Scratch to any position on the Stage with no trouble.

- Every x position on the Stage that's to the right of the center has a positive number.

- Every x position that's to the left of the center has a negative number.

- Every y position that's above the center has a positive number.

- Every y position that's below the center has a negative number.

Figure 2-10 displays a grid that shows you these four rules.

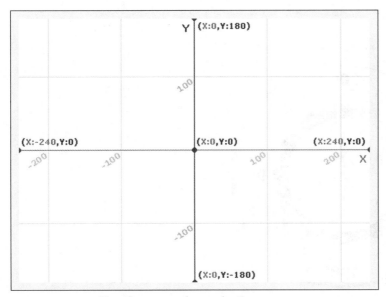

FIGURE 2-10 Visualizing x and y on the Stage

The very top of the Stage has a y value of 180, and the very bottom has a y value of −180. The right edge has an x value of 240 and the left edge has an x value of −240.

VIDEO

To play a coordinates guessing game with Scratch the Cat and Eva, visit the companion website at www.wiley.com/go/adventuresincoding and select Adventure 2!

Knowing Your Directions

Now that you know how to move sprites around on the Stage, the next thing to learn is how to make them turn, or rotate.

When you move a sprite using the `move () steps` block, it always goes in a straight line and moves the number of steps (pixels) that you enter in the oval inside the block. If you want to change the direction that the sprite moves, you need to rotate the sprite to face in a different direction.

To turn a sprite, you need to be familiar with how a compass works. A compass measures directions (East, West, North, and South) using degrees. There are 360 degrees in a complete circle.

North on a compass is 0 degrees. East is 90 degrees. South is 180 degrees. West is 270 degrees. Figure 2-11 shows a compass with the degrees marked on it.

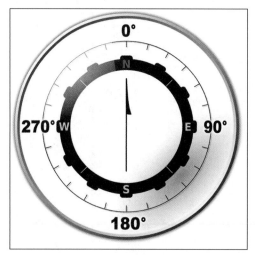

FIGURE 2-11 Degrees of direction on a compass

When you create a new sprite, it always faces toward 90 degrees. If you open the Sprite Info Pane, you can see the direction that the sprite is currently facing by looking at the number to the right of the *x* and *y* positions, as shown in Figure 2-12.

FIGURE 2-12 Sprites start out facing to 90 degrees

The symbol for degrees of direction is the same as the symbol for degrees of temperature. So, when we say 180°, we mean the same thing as 180 degrees.

Working with Degrees of Rotation

Take a look at the Sprite Info Pane again. Just to the right of the current number of degrees that the sprite is facing is a circle with a line in it, as shown in Figure 2-13. This is a handy tool that you can use to change the direction that your sprite is facing.

FIGURE 2-13 The Direction Changing Tool

To use the Direction Changing Tool, just click the line in the circle and drag it to face a different direction. Your sprite also rotates as you drag the line.

Spinning Sprites

Sprites can rotate clockwise or counterclockwise. When they turn clockwise, the degree numbers get larger. When they turn counterclockwise, the degrees get smaller.

To experiment with rotating a sprite, follow these steps:

1. Create a new project by selecting File ⇨ New from the toolbar.

2. Go to the Events Block Palette and drag the when green flag clicked block to the Scripts Area.

3. Go to the Sensing Block Palette and drag the `ask ()  and  wait` block to the Scripts Area. Snap it to the bottom of the `when green flag clicked` block, as shown in Figure 2-14.

FIGURE 2-14 Snapping the `ask ()  and  wait` block to the `when green flag clicked` block

4. Click inside the `ask ()  and  wait` block and change the question to "What direction should I point?," as shown in Figure 2-15.

The `ask ()  and  wait` block asks the user to type text to answer a question. It causes the program to stop running until the user answers the question.

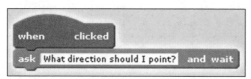

FIGURE 2-15 Changing the question in the `ask ()  and  wait` block

5. Go to the Motion Block Palette and drag the `point in direction ()` block to the Scripts Area.

The `point in direction ()` block changes the direction that the sprite is facing.

6. Go to the Sensing Block Palette and drag the `answer` block to the Scripts Area. Snap it into the oval space inside the `point in direction ()` block, as shown in Figure 2-16.

The `answer` block contains the answer that the user gives to the question that was asked by the `ask ()  and  wait` block.

FIGURE 2-16 Snapping the answer block into the `point in direction ()` block

7. Snap the `point in direction ()` block to the bottom of the `ask ()` and `wait` block, as shown in Figure 2-17.

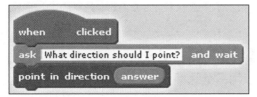

FIGURE 2-17 Snapping the `point in direction ()` block to the bottom of the `ask ()` and `wait` block

8. Click the Green Flag!

   Scratch asks you a question and you see the question and a text input box appear at the bottom of the Stage, as shown in Figure 2-18.

FIGURE 2-18 Running the direction-pointing program

9. Enter a number between 0 and 359 into the text input box.

   The sprite changes directions.

Notice that the maximum number of degrees is 359. That's because 0 is the first number when you're counting degrees. So, 0 and 360 point in exactly the same direction. Try it out!

This is great so far, but right now you have to restart the program every time you want to enter a new direction. Can you guess how to fix this so that Scratch the Cat asks you for a new number immediately after you give her an answer?

If you guessed that the answer is to use a `forever` block, you're right! Go to the Control Block Palette and drag the `forever` block so that it snaps around everything under the `when green flag clicked` block, as shown in Figure 2-19.

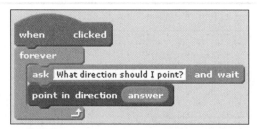

FIGURE 2-19 Looping the direction-pointing program

CHALLENGE

Can you work out how to have Scratch the Cat ask a second question, such as "How far should I move?," and then have her move that distance?

Moving a Sprite

Scratch has several ways to move sprites around the Stage. Depending on how you want your sprites to move, you can choose among stepping, gliding, and jumping.

Stepping

Stepping is what sprites do when you use the move () steps block. Stepping moves a sprite in a straight line for a certain number of pixels (steps) at a time in the direction that the sprite is currently facing. Stepping can look smooth if the steps are small enough, or it can look jagged if you move the sprite in larger sized steps.

Gliding

Gliding moves a sprite in a smooth way from one set of *x* and *y* coordinates to another. You can determine the time that the actual gliding animation takes by entering a number, in seconds, into the block. Gliding doesn't depend at all on the direction that the sprite is facing.

To try out gliding, follow these steps:

1. Drag the glide () secs to x: () y: () block from the Motion Block Palette to the Scripts Area.

   The glide () secs to x: () y: () block is shown in Figure 2-20.

FIGURE 2-20 The glide () secs to x: () y: () block

2. Leave the first oval in the glide block set to 1. This is the number of seconds the glide animation will take.

3. Enter 240 into the *x* input and 180 into the *y* input.

4. Double-click the glide () secs to x: () y: () block.

   The sprite glides across the screen to the upper-right corner of the Stage.

Jumping

You can make your sprites jump from one position on the screen to another without any steps in between by using the go to x: () y: () block. To use the go to x: () y: () block, follow these steps:

1. Drag the go to x: () y: () block from the Motion Block Palette to the Scripts Area.

2. Set the *x* value to –200 and the *y* value to –100.

3. Double-click the `go to x: () y: ()` block.

The sprite disappears from its current location and reappears instantly at the new location.

Creating Random Scratch Art

In this part of the adventure, you create a random straight-line drawing program. The program draws a line from one point to another on the screen and then waits for a second before heading off in a new direction and drawing a new line. The program repeats until you stop it.

To get started, create a new project by selecting File ⇨ New.

Randomizing Movements

In order to draw random lines, you first need to learn to move a sprite to a random location. Follow these steps to create random numbers for *x* and *y* and then put those numbers into a `glide() secs to x: () y: ()` block:

1. Go to the Operators Block Palette and drag the `pick random () to ()` block to the Scripts Area.

   The `pick random () to ()` block looks like Figure 2-21.

FIGURE 2-21 The `pick random () to ()` block

2. Set the first value in the `pick random () to ()` block to –240 and set the second to 240.

   This is your *x* value.

3. Drag another `pick random () to ()` block to the Scripts Area.

4. Set the first value of the new `pick random () to ()` block to –180 and set the second one to 180.

   This is your *y* value.

5. Go to the Motion Block Palette and drag the `glide () secs to x: () y: ()` block to the Scripts Area.

6. Snap the first `pick random () to ()` block (containing –240 to 240) into the *x* value of the `glide () secs to x: () y: ()` block.

7. Snap the second `pick random () to ()` block (containing –180 to 180) into the *y* value of the `glide () secs to x: () y: ()` block.

   After you have fit both `random` blocks into place, your `glide () secs to x: () y: ()` block should look like Figure 2-22.

```
glide 1 secs to x: pick random -240 to 240  y: pick random -180 to 180
```

FIGURE 2-22 The finished random gliding block

You may want to expand your Scripts Area by clicking on the expansion arrow, so you can fully see your code blocks.

8. Double-click the `glide () secs to x: () y: ()` block.

   Scratch glides to a new random location on the Stage.

9. Drag the `when green flag clicked` block from the Events Block Palette to the Scripts Area and snap it to the top of the `glide () secs to x: () y: ()` block.

   Now the sprite glides to a new random location every time you click the Green Flag.

10. Drag the `forever` block from the Control Block Palette and snap it around the `glide () secs to x: () y: ()` block.

11. Drag the `wait () secs` block from the Control Block Palette and snap it underneath the `glide () secs to x: () y: ()` block.

12. Change the value of the `wait () secs` block to 1 second.

    The program should now look like Figure 2-23.

```
when      clicked
forever
    glide 1 secs to x: pick random -240 to 240  y: pick random -180 to 180
    wait 1 secs
```

FIGURE 2-23 The random and repeating glides script

13. Click the Green Flag to see the random and repeating glides.

14. Click the Stop Sign.

Drawing Random Lines

Your next step in creating the program is to make Scratch the Cat draw lines as she moves. To start drawing, follow these steps:

1. Go to the Pen Block Palette and drag the `pen down` block to the Scripts Area. Snap it to the top of the `glide () secs to x: () y: ()` block.

   The `pen` block causes a sprite to draw as it moves. You can think of it as Scratch the Cat holding a pen as she's gliding across the Stage.

2. Click the Green Flag.

   Scratch the Cat starts moving randomly while drawing a line behind her.

So far, so good! But, the lines Scratch the Cat is drawing are all the same color. You can make this more interesting.

Before you get started, click the Stop Sign. Next, drag the `clear` block from the Pen Block Palette to the Scripts Area. Double-click it to clear the lines that Scratch the Cat has drawn so far.

Follow these steps to make the color of the lines change:

1. Drag the `change pen color by ()` block from the Pen Block Palette and snap it to the bottom of the `glide () secs to x: () y: ()` block in your script.

   Your script should now look like Figure 2-24.

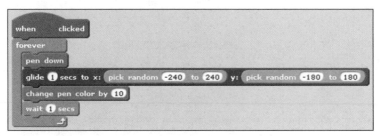

FIGURE 2-24 Drawing random colored lines

2. Click the Green Flag and watch Scratch the Cat draw random, colorful lines!

CHALLENGE

Now that you know how to move sprites around the Stage, try changing and improving (in Scratch, this is called *remixing*) your script with some of these challenge exercises!

- Make the color of the lines change randomly.
- Change the size of the pen randomly with each new line.
- Clear the Stage of all the previously drawn lines every time the Green Flag is clicked, but before the loop starts.
- Make the number of seconds between lines a random value.

Further Adventures in Coding

To learn more about using random movements in Scratch to create games, check out Fish!, a game and tutorial created by Scratch User aaa1001 on the Scratch website at `https://scratch.mit.edu/projects/10559841/`.

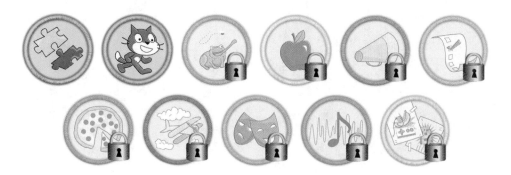

Achievement Unlocked: **Moving around the Stage**

In the Next Adventure

In the next adventure, you learn about using blocks to make decisions and form loops.

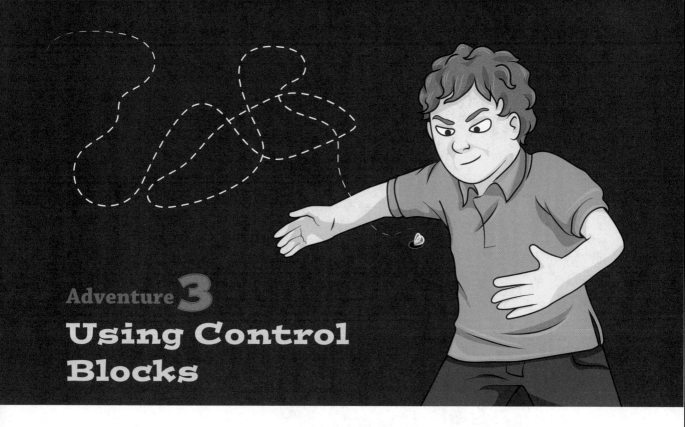

Adventure 3
Using Control Blocks

IN THIS ADVENTURE, you learn about blocks that make decisions and create different kinds of loops besides the simple forever loop that you saw in previous adventures.

Understanding Code Nesting

The blocks you learn about and work with in this adventure are the C-blocks. The `forever` block that you used in the previous adventures is an example of a C-block. C-blocks wrap around other blocks to control when and whether the blocks inside of them are executed.

Figure 3-1 shows an example of a C-block wrapped around a `move () steps` block and a turn `clockwise () degrees` block. Without running this script in Scratch, can you guess what it will do?

Now try building and running the script in Figure 3-1 to see if you were right about what it does! If you guessed that it moves the sprite in a circle, you're right!

When code fits inside of other code like this, programmers call it **nesting**. Think about a bird inside a nest. Now, think about a nest with a nest inside of it, with a nest inside of that, with a bird in that nest. In the bird world, this might never happen, but it happens all the time in programming.

FIGURE 3-1 A C-block

DEFINITIONS
When one block, or piece of code, is inside of another block, it's called **nesting**.

Figure 3-2 shows a C-block nested within another C-block. What do you think this one does when you run it?

```
repeat 4
    play drum 2 for 0.25 beats
    repeat 2
        play drum 1 for 0.25 beats
    play drum 5 for 0.25 beats
```

FIGURE 3-2 Nested C-blocks

In order to figure out what the nested loops do, you can start at the top and follow the loop in your head, as if you're inside the program. Starting at the top, the program in Figure 3-2 does the following:

1. Creates a loop to repeat the following code four times.

2. Plays a drum beat (drum #2, which happens to be a bass drum) for .25 beats.

3. Creates another loop to repeat the following code two times.

4. Plays a drum beat (drum #1, which is the snare drum) for .25 beats.

5. Goes back to the top of the inner loop.

6. Plays a drum (drum #1).

Now that the program went back to the top of the inner loop, the inner loop is finished (because it has looped twice), so the program moves on to the next block.

7. Plays a drumbeat (drum #5, a hi-hat cymbal) for .25 beats.

8. Checks whether the outer loop has repeated four times. If not, goes back to the beginning.

Now try to build this loop and run it for yourself. You can find the `play drum` block in the Sound Block Palette, and the `repeat` blocks are in the Control Block Palette.

After you've built and run this program, does it do what you expected it to do? Can you follow the steps as it runs? If it's going too fast, try changing the number of beats that each drum runs to a larger number to slow it down.

By nesting blocks within C-blocks, you can create complex programs with fewer lines of code. The same program as shown in Figure 3-2 could be created without nesting, but it would take a lot more blocks. Figure 3-3 shows a program that does the exact same thing as the program in Figure 3-2, but without nesting.

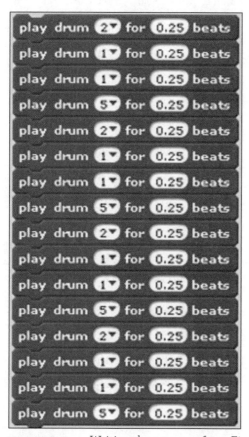

FIGURE 3-3 Writing the program from Figure 3-2 without nesting

Branching Programs in Scratch

You can use C-blocks and nesting for more than just repeating blocks of code. Branching is how you tell a program to make choices between two or more possible paths.

> **DEFINITIONS**
>
> **Branching** is a term that programmers use to describe code that chooses between multiple different paths.

For example, you might write a game in which a character comes to a fork in the road and must choose a path.

This is an example of branching. In English, you might say something like:

> If the road looks less travelled, go down that one.

In Scratch (and every other programming language we know of), you write a branching statement using an if () then block.

The if () then Block

You can find the if () then block inside the Control Block Palette. It looks like Figure 3-4.

FIGURE 3-4 The if () then block

The if () then block is a C-block, so you can nest other blocks inside of it. But it also has a hexagon-shaped space for a Boolean block between the words if and then. This is where you put a block that responds with a True or False answer.

For example, if you want to write a program that plays a sound whenever you press the space bar, you can write that with an if () then block, as shown in Figure 3-5.

The program in Figure 3-5 contains a forever loop that runs when you click the Green Flag. The loop checks over and over to see whether you've pressed the space bar. If so, it plays the "meow" sound. If you never press the space bar, the meow sound never plays.

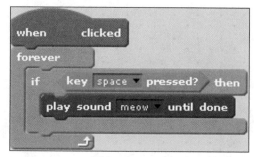

FIGURE 3-5 Playing a sound when the space bar is pressed

What if you want the program to do something else when the space bar isn't being pressed? This is where the `if () then, else` block, which is covered in the next section, comes into play.

The if () then, else Block

The `if () then, else` block works much the same as an `if () then` block. The `if is () then, else` block has a second C-block within it that you can add blocks to that run when the blocks in the `if` section don't run.

Figure 3-6 shows a program that waits for you to press the space bar. If you don't press the space bar, Scratch turns clockwise 15 degrees.

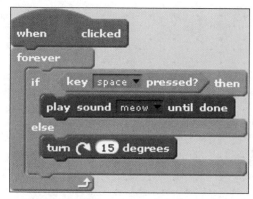

FIGURE 3-6 Demonstrating the `if () then, else` block

You can do so many interesting things with `if () then, else` blocks by nesting other `if () then` and `if () then, else` blocks within them. For example, if you want to play the meow sound when the space bar is pressed, and play a drum when the up-arrow key is pressed, you can nest another `if () then` inside of the `else` C-block, as shown in Figure 3-7.

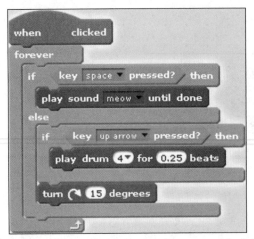

FIGURE 3-7 Nesting an `if () then` block inside of an `if () then, else` block

Things start to get pretty wild (and maybe a little confusing) when you have multiple levels of nesting inside of `if () then` and `if () then, else` blocks. But with practice, you can create some pretty cool things! Figure 3-8 shows how you can use nested `if () then, else` blocks to create a small drum set on your keyboard.

The program in Figure 3-8 checks whether you're pressing any of the arrow keys and plays a different drum for each of them.

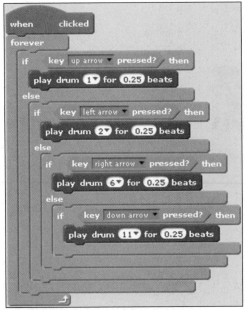

FIGURE 3-8 Creating a keyboard drum set with nested `if () then, else` blocks

There's one big problem with the drum set program in Figure 3-8. Can you guess what it is? The problem is that this drum set only lets you play one drum at a time. Adventure 5 shows you how you can make a more realistic drum set. For now, though, try changing the drum sounds and seeing what sort of fun beats you can come up with!

Boolean Blocks

Any block that can be either true or false is called a **Boolean** block. The `key pressed` block is an example of a Boolean block. The key is either pressed (true) or not pressed (false). There's no "sort of" when it comes to Boolean blocks.

Boolean (which rhymes with "Ghoulian," the name we made up for the language Ghouls speak) is a funny word that means "true or false." Boolean blocks get their name from George Boole, a mathematician who lived in the 1800s.

Scratch's Boolean blocks are kept in two block palettes: the Sensing Block Palette and the Operators Block Palette. You can identify Boolean blocks because they're always hexagon-shaped.

Figure 3-9 shows all the hexagon-shaped blocks in Scratch.

FIGURE 3-9 The hexagon-shaped blocks

There are only 11 hexagon-shaped (Boolean) blocks, but all of them, with the exception of the mouse down? block, contain many different possibilities for determining true or false values in your programs.

You can use only Boolean blocks inside Control blocks that have hexagon spaces. Here's what each Boolean block does:

- touching ()? block. The touching ()? block is true if the sprite is touching whatever you select from its drop-down menu. You can select any other sprite in the program, as well as mouse-pointer and edge. When you select edge, the touching ()? block is true if the sprite is touching the edge of the Stage. When you select mouse-pointer the touching ()? block is true when the mouse pointer is touching the sprite.

- touching color ()?. The touching color ()? block is true if the sprite is touching any object with the color you provide in its color menu.

- color () touching color ()?. The color () touching color ()? block is true if the first color (which is within the sprite) is touching the second color, which may be part of the background or part of another sprite.

- key () pressed?. The key () pressed? block is true when the selected key is pressed.

- mouse down?. The mouse down? block is true when the mouse button is pressed.

- () < (). The () < () block has two spaces for values. It's true when the first value is less than the second one. For example, if you put 10 in the first box and 30 in the second box, then the less than block is true. If you put 30 in the first box and 10 in the second box, the less than block is false.

- () = (). The () = () block is true if the value on the left is the same as the value on the right.

- () > (). The () > () block is true if the value on the left is greater than the value on the right.

- () and (). The () and () block compares the results of two Boolean Blocks and is true if both of the Boolean blocks it contains are true.

- () or (). The () or () block compares the results of two Boolean blocks and is true if one or both of the Boolean blocks is true.

- not (). The not () block reverses whatever Boolean blocks it contains.

Figure 3-10 shows an example use of the not () block. Is the result of the not () block true or false?

FIGURE 3-10 The not () block

If you said that the result of the not () block in Figure 3-10 is true, you're right! Because "apples" is not equal to "oranges," the not () block reports back with a true.

Using not () blocks can be confusing. Fortunately, every not () block can be rewritten as a less mind-bending block. For example, if you want to do something when apples are not equal to oranges, you could use a () = () inside the if part of an if () then, else block. Then, the thing you want the program to do when the condition is false can go inside the else section.

Making Comments in Scratch

As you start building longer programs things can start to get complicated. When you're working on a program, you may completely understand how it works, and you may think that in the future you'll never forget what you were thinking at the time you built them. But, trust us, if you put aside a program you're working on for a few days and come back to it later, you'll often sit there staring and scratching your head trying to figure out what you were doing.

Fortunately Scratch has a way to put notes in your scripts. In programming, notes inside your code that are meant to be read by people, and not by the computer, are called **comments**. Comments are where you can write anything you want to tell yourself or others about the code.

Comments are notes that you leave in a program for your future self or for other coders who may work on the program.

Scratch has two different kinds of comments: standalone comments and block comments.

Standalone Comments

Standalone comments are comments that you add to your script but that aren't connected to any blocks or code in particular. Figure 3-11 shows an example of a standalone comment that we added to the keyboard drum set program.

Standalone comments are great for describing the whole program, as in Figure 3-11. You can also use them to give instructions on how to use the program, or how to play a game, or to remind yourself about improvements that you want to make to a program in the future.

To make a comment, right-click in the Scripts Area and select Add Comment. A new yellow note appears. You can drag a comment anywhere in the Scripts Area, and you can resize it by dragging its lower-right corner.

If you add several comments to your program, your Scripts Area can start to look cluttered. Fortunately, you can make comments smaller by clicking on the arrow in the top-left corner of the comment. Clicking the arrow on a comment "collapses" it so that it takes up less space, but you need to click the arrow again if you want to read it.

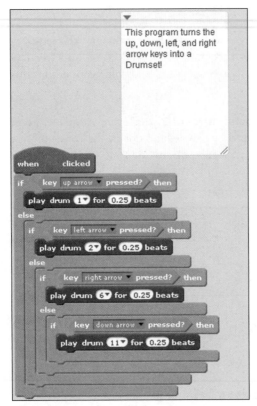

FIGURE 3-11 A standalone comment

Figure 3-12 shows what a collapsed comment looks like.

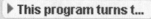

FIGURE 3-12 A collapsed comment

Block Comments

You can also attach comments to blocks in the Scripts Area. When a comment is connected to a block, it's called a block comment.

Block comments are useful for explaining what a particular block or group of blocks does. For example, Figure 3-13 shows the drum set program with block comments added to show at a glance what each part does.

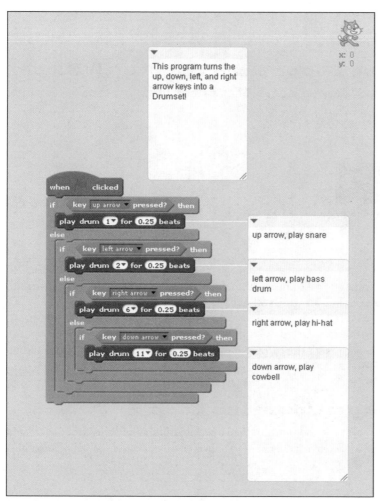

FIGURE 3-13 Using block comments

Looping in Scratch

You've already seen a couple different kinds of loops. In this section, you take a closer look at how to get totally loopy in Scratch.

Looping Forever

The `forever` loop is the simplest type of loop. To use it, just drag it to your Scripts Area and put some blocks inside it to make those blocks loop forever until you stop it. There are several ways to stop a `forever` loop:

- Press the Stop Sign next to the Green Flag.

- Close the browser window where the program is running, or simply go to a different web page.

- Turn off your computer.

- Use the `stop ()` block.

Stopping Loops with the stop () Block

The `stop ()` block, shown in Figure 3-14, stops the running of a script, or of multiple scripts.

FIGURE 3-14 The `stop ()` block

Notice that the `stop ()` block has a flat edge on the bottom. Because its purpose is to end the script, it doesn't make any sense to put anything after it. So, the flat edge indicates that it's not possible to attach other blocks to its bottom.

The drop-down menu in a `stop ()` block lets you choose whether the `stop ()` block stops all the scripts for the current sprite, just part of it, or all the scripts running in the current sprite.

Creating a Counting Loop

Counting loops repeat the code within them a certain number of times. They're created by using the `repeat ()` block. Figure 3-15 shows what a `repeat ()` block looks like.

FIGURE 3-15 The `repeat ()` block

Notice that the `repeat ()` block has an oval in it. You can put a number into the oval, or you can put any of the oval-shaped blocks inside it. Figure 3-16 shows the use of an oval-shaped block inside of a `repeat ()` block.

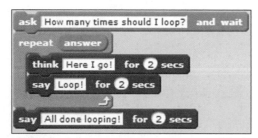

FIGURE 3-16 Using the `repeat ()` block

The program in Figure 3-16 causes Scratch the Cat to ask the users how many times they want the loop to run. It then uses that number to loop the program that number of times! Pretty cool, eh?

Looping Until a Condition Is Met

The final type of loop is called a conditional loop. It's created using the `repeat until ()` block, which is shown in Figure 3-17.

FIGURE 3-17 The `repeat until ()` block

The `repeat until ()` block uses a Boolean block inside of it to determine whether it should stop looping.

Figure 3-18 shows a program that creates a loop that makes Scratch the Cat move and say "Going for a walk!" until she runs into the edge of the Stage.

FIGURE 3-18 Looping with the `repeat until ()` block

Waiting

When loops run too fast, or when you want something to wait for something else to happen in your program, you can use the `wait` blocks. Scratch has two `wait` blocks:

- `wait () secs`. Waits a specified number of seconds (or a fraction of a second).
- `wait until ()`. Waits until a condition is true.

Both `wait` blocks cause the running of the current script to sit there and do nothing for a while. We might hate waiting, but Scratch doesn't mind a bit. Situations when you might want a script to wait include the following:

- To create a pause between movements
- To have a sprite in a game wait until a key is pressed before proceeding with what it was doing
- To pause a script whenever a "pause" button is clicked in a music-player script

Can you think of other times when you might want to pause a script?

Building the Fly Catcher Game

There's nothing better than sitting on a warm rock by the river and catching flies with your tongue. At least, that's what we've been told by frogs.

In this adventure, you create a game where you're a frog that's trying to catch the tastiest of tasty treats: the hippo-fly.

The finished game looks something like Figure 3-19.

Looks like fun, right? Let's get started! Follow these steps to get ready to code:

1. Go to `http://scratch.mit.edu` and click the Create tab at the top of the screen.

2. Give your project a name by clicking inside the input area just above the Stage.

   Call it something like "Fly Catching Adventure" or "Fun Fly Catching."

3. Remove Scratch the Cat from the Stage by using the Delete tool from the toolbar, or by right-clicking on her and selecting Delete.

Now you're ready to go! Move on to the next section to set up the backdrop.

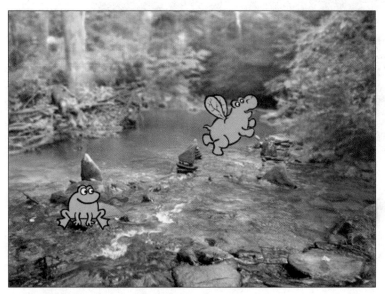

FIGURE 3-19 The finished Fly Catcher game

Setting the Stage

Our scene begins in a peaceful stream in the forest. But, all we have now is a polar bear in a snowstorm. Follow these steps to set the backdrop.

1. Click the first icon in the row of icons under New Backdrop in the lower-left corner of the Project Editor.

   The Backdrop Library opens.

2. Click Outdoors in the left menu of the Backdrop Library and find the backdrop named Water and Rocks.

3. Click the Water and Rocks backdrop and click the OK button to set it as a backdrop for the current project.

Your Stage should now look like Figure 3-20.

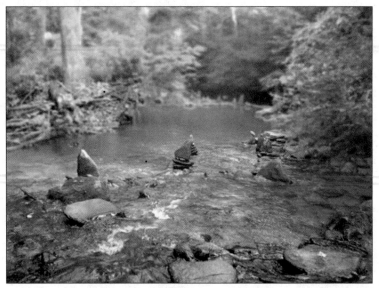

FIGURE 3-20 The Water and Rocks backdrop

Placing the Frog

It's time to bring in the star of our game—the frog. Follow these steps to add a frog sprite:

1. Click the first icon in the New Sprite menu to open the Sprite Library.

2. Locate the Frog sprite, click it, and click OK.

   The frog is added to the center of the Stage.

3. Drag the frog to position it on a nice fly-catching rock in the stream, like that one toward the left.

That's all for the frog! All the action in this game takes place through the hippo-fly sprite and through a sprite that you create for the frog's tongue.

Adding the Hippo-Fly

Now it's time for the hippo-fly. Follow these steps to add him to the Stage.

1. Open the Sprite Library and locate the flying hippo in the Animals category.

2. Click the hippo and click OK to add it to the Stage.

3. Click the Shrink tool in the toolbar and use it to make the hippo smaller. (A smaller hippo-fly will make the game more of a challenge.)

That's all there is to it! You now have the two main characters on set and ready to go, as shown in Figure 3-21. Next up, you add some action!

FIGURE 3-21 The frog and hippo are on the Stage!

To watch Eva build the complete Fly Catcher Game, visit the companion website at `www.wiley.com/go/adventuresincoding` and select the Adventure 3 video.

Scripting the Hippo-Fly

The hippo-fly's only job in this game is to fly around as fast as he can, in random directions. Here's how to make him do that:

1. Click on the hippo in the Sprite Pane.

2. Drag the when green flag clicked block to the Scripts Area.

3. Drag a forever loop to the Scripts Area and snap it to the when green flag clicked block.

4. Inside the forever loop, drag a move () steps block.

5. Change the value in the move () steps block to 30.

6. Drag a turn clockwise () degrees block to the Scripts Area and snap it to the bottom of the move () steps block.

7. Click into the Operators Block Palette and drag a pick random () to () block into the turn clockwise () degrees block.

8. Set the values in the pick random () to () block to 1 and 10.

9. Drag an if on edge, bounce block to the Scripts Area and snap it to the turn clockwise () degrees block.

Your finished script for the hippo-fly should look like Figure 3-22. Check your work carefully before moving on.

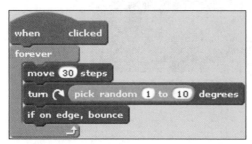

FIGURE 3-22 The flying script for the hippo-fly

Making the Tongue

You may have noticed that the frog's tongue is always sticking out. It wouldn't be much of a game if you programmed it to just wait until the hippo-fly happens to run into the tongue. To add an element of skill to the game, you'll give the frog an extra-long tongue that shows up only when you press the space bar.

Follow these steps to create the tongue and to make it appear when the space bar is pressed.

1. Click the icon that looks like a paintbrush in the New Sprite toolbar.

    The Paint Editor opens.

2. Change the color for the brush to red by clicking red in the Color Palette at the bottom of the Paint Editor.

3. Change the width of the paintbrush to something around the same width as the frog's existing tongue, by sliding the Brush Size Bar.

4. Start at the edge of the canvas and draw a curvy tongue, as shown in Figure 3-23.

    The tongue appears on the Stage as you draw it.

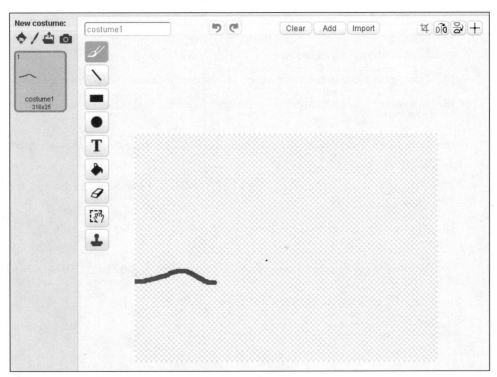

FIGURE 3-23 Drawing a curvy tongue

5. Click and drag the tongue on the Stage to move it into position so that it covers up the existing tongue on the frog.

    You may need to redraw or tweak your new tongue so that it fits.

6. Click the *i* icon on the tongue sprite to open the Sprite Info Pane.

7. Change the name of the sprite to Frog Tongue, and uncheck the box next to the word Show.

   The tongue disappears from the Stage.

8. Switch to the Scripts Area by clicking the Scripts tab at the top of the Project Editor.

9. With the tongue selected in the Sprite Pane, find the `when key () pressed` block in the Events Block Palette and drag it to the Scripts Area.

10. Make sure that space is selected in the `when key () pressed` block.

11. Drag the `show block` from the Looks Block Palette and snap it to the `when () key pressed` block.

12. Drag an `if () then, else` block to the Scripts Area and snap it to the bottom of the `show` block.

13. Drag the `touching ()` block from the Sensing Block Palette and drag it into the `if () then, else` block.

14. Change the value in the `touching ()` block to the name of the hippo sprite.

15. Drag a `say ()` block from the Looks Block Palette to inside the `if` part of the `if () then, else` block.

16. Drag another `say ()` block from the Looks Block Palette to inside the `else` part of the `if () then, else` block.

17. Change the words that the frog says when he catches or misses the fly to whatever you want him to say.

18. Drag a `hide` block from the Looks Block Palette to the bottom of the `if () then, else` block.

   This makes the tongue go away after the fly is caught or not caught.

The finished frog tongue script should look like Figure 3-24.

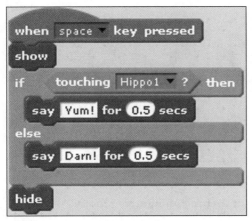

FIGURE 3-24 The finished frog tongue script

Now it's time to try it out! Click the Green Flag and see if everything works as it should.

CHALLENGE

Now that the basic Fly Catcher game is done, we have some ideas for how to improve it. Try out any or all of these!

- Add comments to the code to explain how it works.
- Have the tongue make a noise when it catches (or doesn't catch) the hippo-fly.
- Pause the game and show a "winner!" message after the frog catches the fly three times.
- Move the frog to a new random location on the Stage after each catch.

Further Adventures in Coding

To advance your knowledge of coding using loops, read our article "Advanced Looping with JavaScript" at www.dummies.com/how-to/content/advanced-looping-with-javascript.html.

Achievement Unlocked: Branching and getting loopy

In the Next Adventure

In the next adventure, you find out how you can write code to detect and respond to actions in the real world, such as mouse movements, typing on the keyboard, and even movements in front of a camera!

Adventure 4

Using Sensing Blocks

LEARNING SCRATCH (OR any other language, for that matter) is all about discovering and finding out new things. In the real world, you use your five senses to find out new things. In the Scratch world, you use a category of blocks called the *sensing blocks*.

In this adventure, you see how to use the sensing blocks to detect things such as typing on the keyboard, mouse movements, and more!

You've already learned about using sensing blocks to detect key presses in Adventure 3's drum set program. The Sensing Block Palette contains many other blocks.

Learning the Sensing Blocks

The Sensing Block Pallet contains 20 blocks, as shown in Figure 4-1. These blocks are colored light blue. There are 4 stack blocks, 5 Boolean blocks, and 11 reporter blocks.

Sensing blocks can be used for a number of different things. They can be used to keep track of how long things take within your program. They can be used to ask questions and then store the answers to be used within other blocks, and they can also be used to detect whether a key has been pressed on your keyboard or if there's been movement of your mouse.

You can also use Sensing blocks to detect whether your sprite is touching something, how far away from another sprite it is, or where a sprite is on the Stage.

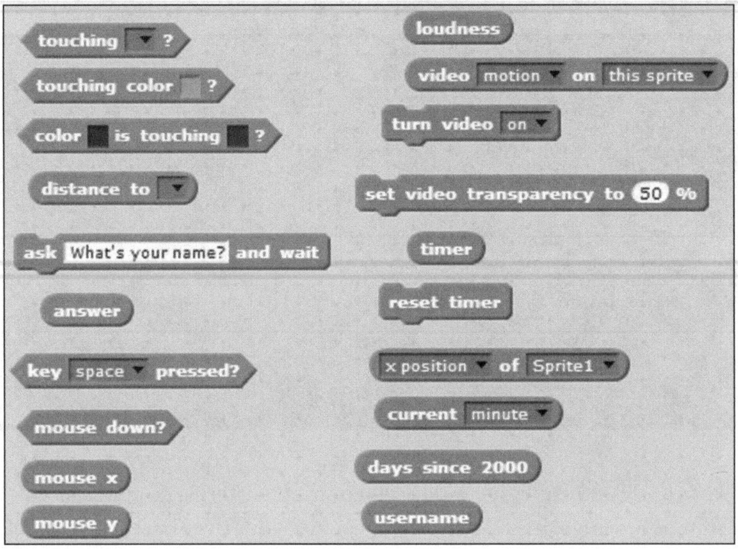

FIGURE 4-1 The sensing blocks

Sensing blocks tell your project what's going on so that it can do things in response.

CHALLENGE

Can you tell by looking at the blocks in Figure 4-1 which category they go into? Write an "S" next to each stack block, a "B" next to each Boolean block, and an "R" next to each of the reporter blocks. If you need a refresher on what each of these blocks look like, check the glossary!

Getting and Using Text Input

When you type words or numbers using your keyboard, that's known as "text input" to Scratch. The `ask ()` and `wait` block, shown in Figure 4-2, is how you make a sprite ask for text input.

FIGURE 4-2 The `ask () and wait` block

When you use an `ask () and wait` block in your project, it causes a sprite to ask a question. A text input area appears at the bottom of the Stage, as shown in Figure 4-3.

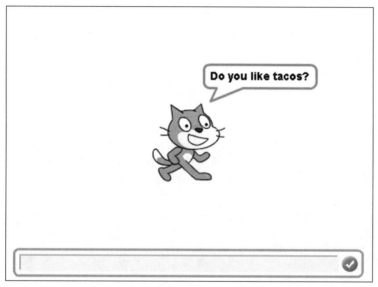

FIGURE 4-3 Scratch the Cat wants to know something.

Even though it's called an "ask" and wait block, you can type any message you want to display. You may sometimes want to use it to prompt a user for an answer without asking a question, such as `Enter Your Name`.

When you're done typing your answer, click the checkmark on the right of the text input or press Enter (or Return on a Mac) to **submit** your text input to Scratch.

DEFINITIONS

To **submit** input means to send the words or numbers you typed into a text box to the program that asked you a question. Before you submit the input, the script doesn't know what you typed and can't do anything with it.

When you submit input, the value from the input area gets put into another sensing block, the `answer` block, which you can see in Figure 4-4.

FIGURE 4-4 The `answer` block

The `answer` block stores whatever value you put into the text input area. You can then use the `answer` block to make different things happen. Follow these steps to create a simple **chat bot** program that uses the `ask and wait` and `answer` blocks to ask questions and store answers.

DEFINITIONS

A **chat bot** is a computer program that talks, or chats, with people.

1. Select New from the File menu in the Project Editor to create a new project.

2. Drag a `when green flag clicked` block from the Events Block Palette to the Scripts Area.

3. Drag the `ask () and wait` block from the Sensing Block Palette to the Scripts Area.

4. Change the text in the `ask () and wait` box to **What's your favorite programming language?**

5. Drag an `if () then, else` block from the Control Block Palette and snap it to the bottom of the `ask () and wait` block.

6. Drag the `() = ()` block from the Operators Block Palette and drop it into the space after `if` in the `if () then, else` block.

   Your Scripts Area should now look like Figure 4-5.

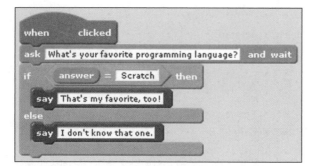

FIGURE 4-5 The () = () block inside of the if () then, else block

7. Drag the answer block from the Sensing Block Palette and drop it into the first space in the () = () block.

    Notice that even though the () = () block's open spaces are squares, you can still drop oval-shaped blocks into them.

8. Click in the second block and type the word **Scratch**.

9. Drag the say () block from the Looks Block Palette and drop it into the space after the then in the if () then, else block.

10. Change the value in the say () block to **That's my favorite, too!**

11. Drag another say () block to the Scripts Area and drop it into the space after the else in the if () then, else block.

12. Change the value of this say () block to **I don't know that one.**

    Your Scripts Area should now look like Figure 4-6.

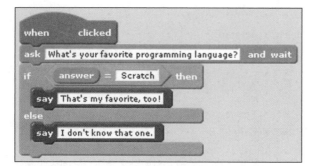

FIGURE 4-6 The beginning of a simple chat bot

Next, you make the chat bot more personable by having Scratch the Cat greet you. Follow these steps.

1. Drag an `ask ()` and `wait` block from the Sensing Block Palette and snap it to the bottom of the `when green flag clicked` block.

   Leave the value in this block set to What's your name?

2. Drag a `say () for () secs` block from the Looks Block Palette and snap it to the bottom of the block that asks for your name.

3. Drag a `join () ()` block from the Operators Block Palette and drop it into the `say () for () secs` block.

4. Drag an `answer` block from the Sensing Block Palette and drop it into the second space in the `join` block.

   Your script should now look like Figure 4-7.

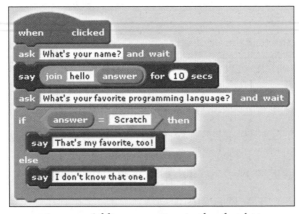

FIGURE 4-7 Adding a greeting to the chat bot

Now click the Green Flag and chat with Scratch!

CHALLENGE

Here are some ideas for other things to add to the chat bot. Add another question that asks for your age and then give a different response depending on whether the age is under 10 or over 10. Nest an `if () then` block inside the `else` part of the first `if () then, else` block to say "That's a good one!" if you enter JavaScript as your favorite programming language. Create a loop that starts the program over after all the questions have been asked. Use a `while` loop instead of the `if () then, else` block to keep asking for the favorite programming language until the answer is Scratch.

To watch Chris complete some of the additions to the Chat Bot program, visit the companion website at www.wiley.com/go/adventuresincoding and choose Adventure 4.

Detecting Key Presses

Typing text is just one of the things you can do with the keyboard. If you've ever played a game on your computer that uses the keyboard, you know that you're not always typing numbers or words in answer to questions.

The `key () pressed` block detects when a key is pressed. With this block, you can make a space ship fire its rockets when you press the space bar, or turn left and right with the arrow keys.

Follow these steps to make a helicopter that moves up and down when you press the arrow keys.

1. Make a new project by selecting File ⇨ New from the top menu.

2. Click the Choose Sprite from Library icon in the New Sprite toolbar at the top of the Sprites Pane.

    The Sprite Library opens.

3. Locate the Helicopter sprite in the transportation category, as shown in Figure 4-8.

FIGURE 4-8 The helicopter sprite

4. Select the Helicopter sprite and click OK to add it to the Sprites Pane.

5. Select the Scratch the Cat sprite and remove it from the project by right-clicking it and selecting Delete, or by using the Delete tool from the top menu.

6. Drag a `when green flag clicked` block from the Events Block Palette to the Scripts Area.

7. Drag a `forever` block from the Control Block Palette and snap it to the `when green flag clicked` block.

8. Drag two `if () then` blocks from the Control Block Palette and place them inside the `forever` block.

9. Drag two `key () pressed` blocks to the Scripts Area and drop them into each of the `if () then` blocks.

10. Change the value of the first `key () pressed` block to `up arrow`.

11. Change the value of the second `key () pressed` block to `down arrow`.

12. Drag two `change y by ()` blocks from the Motion Block Palette and place them inside each of the `if () then` blocks.

13. Change the value of the second `change y by ()` block from 10 to **–10**.

Your Scripts Area should now look like Figure 4-9.

FIGURE 4-9 The up and down helicopter script

Click the Green Flag and then press the up and down arrows on your keyboard. The helicopter goes up and down, depending on which key you press.

> If your keyboard doesn't have up and down arrows, choose different keys to represent the up and down arrows. For example, you might use the Q and A keys, or any other two.

Can you figure out how to add blocks to the script to make the helicopter move left and right when you press the left- and right-arrow keys (or any other two keys)?

Watching for Mouse Moves

When you move or click your mouse, or use a touchpad, Scratch can sense that too by using the `mouse down?`, `mouse x`, and `mouse y` blocks! Here's how to change the helicopter script so that you can control the position of the helicopter using a mouse.

1. Start with the finished helicopter script, which is shown in Figure 4-10.

    If your script doesn't look like this, take a moment to make it match. Figure 4-10 also contains the answer to the previous challenge.

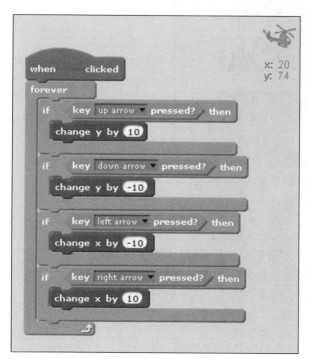

FIGURE 4-10 The finished helicopter script

2. Drag the `if () then, else` block so that it surrounds the `if () then` block in the Scripts Area, as shown in Figure 4-11.

To make sure that it's in the right place, position it so that it snaps inside of the `forever` block.

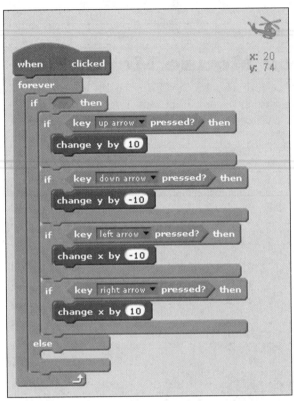

FIGURE 4-11 Adding another `if () then, else` block

3. Drag the `if () then, else` block containing the arrow key commands from the `then` part into the `else` part, as shown in Figure 4-12.

4. Drag a `mouse down?` block from the Sensing Block Palette and drop it into the new `if () then, else` block.

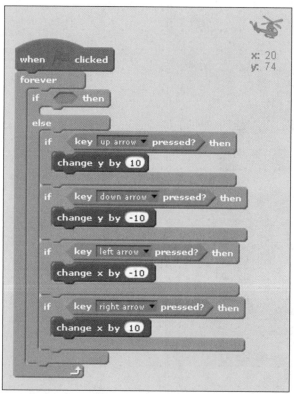

FIGURE 4-12 Moving the keyboard commands to the else section

5. Drag a go to x: () y: () block into the then part of your if () then, else block.

6. Drop a mouse x block from the Sensing Block Palette into the x: () part of the go to x: () y: () block and a mouse y block into the y: () part.

   The final program should look like Figure 4-13.

Click the Green Flag. Click anywhere on the Stage, and the helicopter will instantly move to that spot.

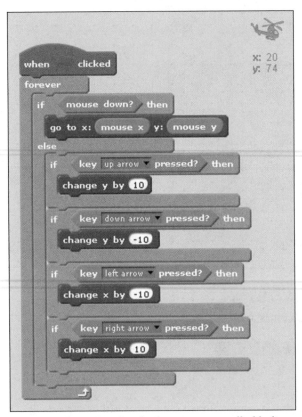

FIGURE 4-13 The finished mouse-controlled helicopter script

CHALLENGE

Can you make the helicopter move in a smooth way to the place where you click your mouse, rather than jumping right to it?

Using Timing

The `timer` block keeps track of time. You can use the timer to make things happen in your scripts after a certain amount of time, or find out how many seconds it takes a user to do something.

One game you can build with the timer is a game where you guess the number of seconds that have happened since the Green Flag was clicked. To build this game, follow these steps.

1. Create a new project by selecting File ⇨ New.

2. Drag a when green flag clicked block to the Scripts Area.

3. Drag a reset timer block from the Sensing Block Palette to the Scripts Area, and snap it to the bottom of the when green flag clicked block.

   This reset timer block resets the timer to 0 when you click the Green Flag.

4. Drag a say () block from the Looks Block Palette and change the words to **Press the space bar in between 5 and 10 seconds!**

5. Drag a forever block from the Control Block Palette to the Scripts Area and snap it to the bottom of the say () block.

6. Drag an if () then block to the stage and snap it to the forever block.

7. Drag a key () pressed? block into the hexagonal space in the if () then block.

8. Make sure that the value in the key () pressed block is space.

   At this point, your Scripts Area should look like Figure 4-14.

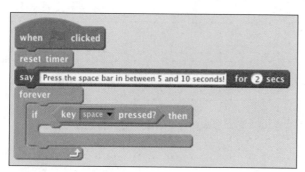

FIGURE 4-14 The first half of the timer game

In the next part, you create the code that checks whether the space bar was pressed in between 5 and 10 seconds. Follow these steps.

1. Drag an if () then, else block inside the if () then block in the Scripts Area.

2. Drag a () and () block from the Operators Block Palette to the Scripts Area.

   Don't snap this block into any other blocks at this point. The () and () block test two different things and produces TRUE if both of the tests produce TRUE.

3. Drag a `() > ()` block into the first space in the `() and ()` block.

   This block checks whether the first value is greater than the second one and produces TRUE if so.

4. Drag a `() < ()` block into the second space in the `() and ()` block.

   This block checks whether the first value is less than the second one and produces TRUE if so.

5. Drag the `timer` block from the Sensing Blocks Palette into the first opening in the `() > ()` block.

6. Change the number in the second part of the first `() > ()` block to the number **5.**

7. Drag another `timer` block from the Sensing Blocks Palette into the first opening of the `() > ()` block.

8. Change the number in the second part of the second `() < ()` block to **10.**

Can you see how this rather complicated block will work? It looks at two statements, `timer > 5` and `timer < 10`, and returns TRUE only if both of these statements are TRUE.

9. Drag the completed `() and ()` block into the hexagonal space in the `if ()` `then, else` block.

   Your Scripts Area should now look like Figure 4-15.

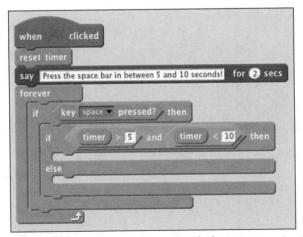

FIGURE 4-15 The timer game with the timer test in place

The last part of the timer game is the part that tells the users whether they were successful in pressing the space bar at the right time. Follow these steps to finish the program!

1. Drag a `say ()` block from the Looks Block Palette into the first section of the `if () then, else` block, after the word `then`.

2. Change the value of the `say ()` block to **Good Job!**

3. Drag another `say ()` block to the Scripts Area and snap it into the `else` part of the `if () then, else` block.

4. Change the value of this `say ()` block to **Nope! Not quite right!**

   When finished, your Scripts Area should look like Figure 4-16.

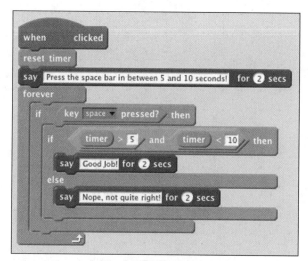

FIGURE 4-16 The finished timer guessing game

Click the Green Flag, count in your head to five, and then press the space bar. How did you do? If you were able to win the game with ease, try changing it so that you have to guess a number between 7 and 10!

Sensing Touching and Distance

Besides detecting input from the keyboard, mouse, and timer, the sprites in Scratch can also detect other sprites and colors on the stage by using the `touching ()` block, the `touching color ()` block, and the `distance to ()` block.

One cool use for the `touching color ()` block is to create a maze. Here's how you can do it!

1. Select File ➪ New to create a new project.

2. Click the Paint Brush icon in the Backdrop Pane to open the Paint Editor and create a new backdrop.

3. Select any color from the Color Palette.

4. Use the Rectangle tool to draw a large rectangle, as shown in Figure 4-17.

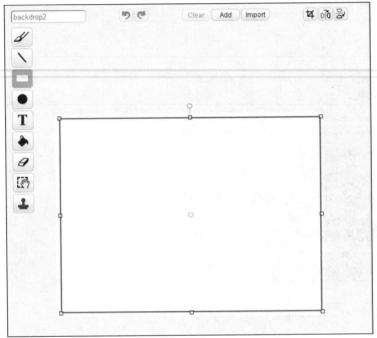

FIGURE 4-17 Draw a rectangle to start the maze backdrop

5. Select the Line tool and use the same color to draw a maze inside the rectangle.

 TIPS & TRICKS   Hold down the Shift key while you draw lines to force them to be straight.

The maze we created is shown in Figure 4-18.

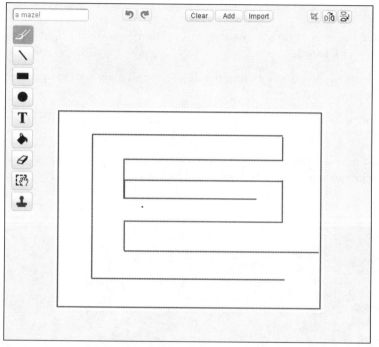

FIGURE 4-18 A maze backdrop

The next step in creating the maze game is to shrink the sprite to a size where she can fit through the maze and to add the code that moves the sprite around the screen when you press the arrow keys.

1. Click the Scripts tab to close the Paint Editor and Backdrop menu.

2. Select the Shrink tool from the top menu and use it to shrink Scratch the Cat to a size where she'll fit inside the maze.

3. Drag a `when green flag clicked` block from the Events Block Palette to the Scripts Area.

4. Drag a `forever` block from the Control Block Palette to the Scripts Area and snap it to the `when green flag clicked` block.

5. Drag four `if () then` blocks from the Control Block Palette to inside of the `forever` block.

6. Drag a `key () pressed?` block from the Sensing Block Palette to the hexagon shape in each of the four `if () then` blocks.

7. Set the keys for the four `key () pressed?` blocks to the four arrow keys: up, down, left, and right (or any four keys of your choice).

8. Drag a `change x by ()` block into the `if () then` block for the left arrow and set its value to **−1**.

9. Drag a `change x by ()` block into the `if () then` block for the right arrow and change its value to **1**.

10. Drag a `change y by ()` block into the `if () then` block for the up arrow and change its value to **1**.

11. Drag a `change y by ()` block into the `if () then` block for the down arrow and set its value to **−1**.

You should now be able to click the Green Flag and move your sprite around with the arrow keys. Your Scripts Area should look similar to Figure 4-19.

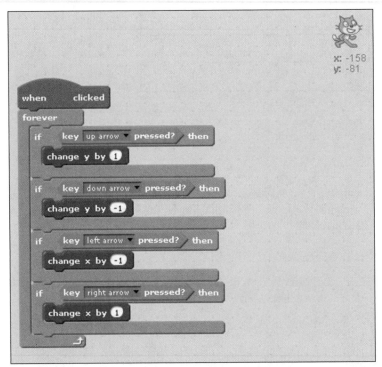

FIGURE 4-19 The maze with the arrow key movement configured

Now you can move a sprite around the screen using the arrow keys, but it's not really a maze because you can still go anywhere on the stage you want to go. Follow these steps to contain the sprite within the maze.

1. Drag an if () then block and snap it inside of the if () then block containing the key (up arrow) pressed? block.

2. Drag a touching color ()? block from the Sensing Block Palette and drop it inside the hexagon shape in the new if () then block.

3. Set the color inside the touching color () block to the same color that you used to draw the maze by clicking the color in the touching color () block and then clicking the wall of your maze.

If the walls of your maze are thin, it can sometimes be a little tricky to select the right color for the touching color () block. Make sure that you get the right one, or else your program won't work correctly.

4. Drag a change y by () block from the Motion Block Palette and snap it inside the if (touching color ()?) block.

5. Change the value in the change y by () block to **–1**.

6. Repeat Steps 1 through 4 for each of the other three arrow keys.

   Make sure that the up and down arrow keys have change y by () blocks and that the left and right arrow keys have change x by () blocks. Make sure all of your x: and y: values match the values in Figure 4-20.

   Your finished script should look like Figure 4-20.

7. Click and drag your sprite to the beginning of the maze and click the Green Flag.

You should now be able to move the sprite through the maze. If it gets stuck, you may need to make the sprite smaller or make the maze bigger. To save your maze, give it a title and click File ⇨ Save.

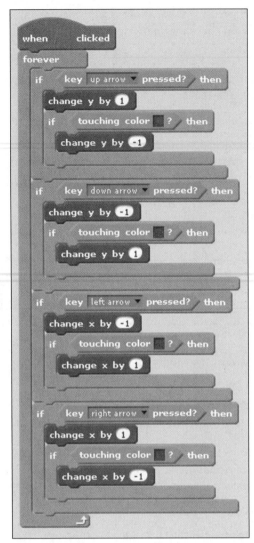

FIGURE 4-20 A working maze app

Building the Apple Patrol Game

In this project, you take the maze game that you created in the last section and make it into a game where you need to navigate a sprite through a maze to get to a final goal as quickly as possible.

To build the game, follow these steps:

1. Open the maze game in the Project Editor and select File ⇨ Save as a Copy from the top menu.

2. Rename the new project **Apple Patrol**.

3. Click the Choose Sprite from Library icon in the New Sprite menu above the Sprite Pane to open the Sprite Library.

4. Locate the Apple sprite and add it to your project.

5. Position the Apple sprite at the end of your maze by dragging it within the stage.

6. Use the Shrink tool in the top menu to make the Apple sprite fit between the walls of the maze, as shown in Figure 4-21.

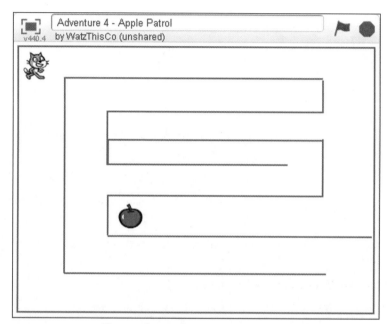

FIGURE 4-21 Placing the apple

7. Select the Apple sprite in the Sprite Pane.

   A new, blank Scripts Area appears.

8. Drag a when green flag clicked block from the Events Block Palette to the Scripts Area.

9. Drag a say () for () secs block from the Looks Block Palette to the Apple's Scripts Area and snap it to the when green flag clicked block.

10. Change the text in the say () for () secs block to **How fast can you find me?**

11. Drag another say () for () secs block from the Looks Block Palette to the Scripts Area and snap it to the first say () for () secs block.

12. Change the text of this block to **Ready?**

13. Add another say () for () secs block and change the text to **Set?**

14. Add another say () for () secs block and change the text to **Go!**

15. Drag a reset timer block from the Sensing Block Palette and snap it to the last say () for () secs block.

16. Drag a forever block from the Control Block Palette and snap it to the bottom of the reset timer block.

17. Snap an if () then block inside the forever block.

18. Snap the touching () block from the Sensing Block Palette into the hexagon shape in the if () then block.

19. Change the value in the touching () block to Sprite 1 (or the name of the Scratch the Cat sprite, if you've changed it).

20. Drag a play sound () block from the Sound Block Palette into the if () then block.

    You can leave the sound set to the default "pop" sound or change it to another.

21. Drag a say () block from the Looks Block Palette and snap it to the play sound () block.

22. Drag a join () () block from the Operators Block Palette and snap it into the say () block.

23. Type **Seconds you took:** into the first box in the join () () block.

24. Drag a timer block from the Sensing Block Palette and drop it into the second box in the join () () block.

25. Drag a stop () block from the Control Block Palette and snap it to the bottom of the say () block.

    When you've finished the script for the Apple sprite, it should look like Figure 4-22.

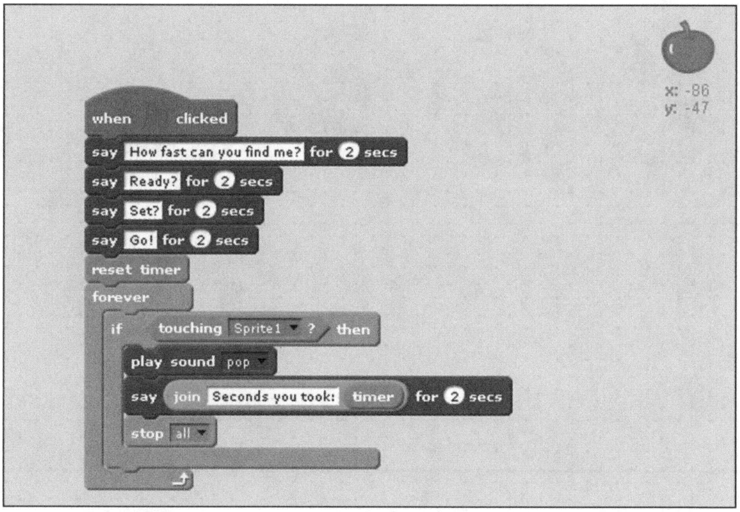

FIGURE 4-22 The Apple sprite's script

There's one last thing you should do before this game is ready to go: Put Scratch the Cat back at the starting line every time the game is started. Follow these steps to make that happen!

1. Click Scratch the Cat in the Sprite Pane to view her Scripts Area.

2. Use your mouse to drag Scratch the Cat across the stage to the place where you want her to start each game.

3. Drag a `go to x: () y: ()` block from the Motion Block Palette and snap it just under the `when green flag clicked` block.

   The coordinates of the current spot where Scratch the Cat is sitting on the stage are already filled in for you, so there's no need to change them!

That will just about do it! Click the Green Flag to try playing the game!

Further Adventures in Coding

The ultimate goal of people who create chat bot programs is to make the chat bot appear to be as human as possible. One way they test this is by using the Turing Test. Visit the link here: `http://www.cnet.com/videos/what-is-the-turing-test/` to watch a video explaining the Turing Test.

Achievement Unlocked: **Using Scratch's A-maze-ing Sensing Blocks!**

In the Next Adventure

The next adventure introduces you to events, which give you a whole different way of programming in Scratch without having to use so much looping!

Adventure 5
Using Event Blocks

IN REAL LIFE, events can be anything that happens, such as a birthday party, parade, or a snowstorm. In programming, **events** are things that happen within your program. Scratch has a special collection of blocks for you to use to make things happen in your programs: the Events Block Palette. You've already seen one such block—the `when green flag clicked` block. In this adventure, you learn about the other Event blocks.

In Scratch, **events** are used to start scripts and broadcast messages in response to things that happen inside and outside of your program.

Understanding the Role of Events

Until now, all your Scratch programming adventures have used `forever` loops to repeatedly check whether an event such as a mouse click or a key press is happening. This method works, but it makes it difficult to keep your code and your Scripts Areas organized.

In this adventure, you learn to use Event blocks to detect things that happen within your program.

There are eight blocks in the Events Block Palette. Six of the Event blocks are **hat blocks**. The other two are **stack blocks**. Event blocks are color-coded brown.

Remember from Adventure 1: A **hat block** is a block that is curved at the top. Hat blocks trigger the start of a script. **Stack blocks** are the rectangular blocks that can be snapped together like puzzle pieces.

Figure 5-1 shows all the Event blocks.

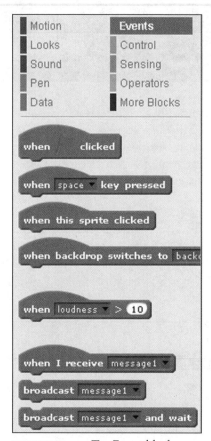

FIGURE 5-1 The Event blocks

Event blocks are an essential part of every Scratch project. With Event blocks, you can do the following:

- Start scripts when keys are pressed, or when sound or movement is detected
- Activate actions when sprites are clicked
- Trigger activities when the Stage's backdrop changes
- Coordinate sprites by sending messages between them
- Get things moving when the Green Flag is clicked

Are you seeing the pattern? Events are the key to making things happen in Scratch!

Although Scratch has been around for more than 12 years, the Events Block Palette is pretty new. Prior to version 2.0, Event blocks were considered Control blocks. In the early days of Scratch 2.0, the blocks we now know as Event blocks were called Trigger blocks.

Working with Key Press Events

In previous adventures, you used loops and `if () then, else` blocks to tell Scratch to watch for key presses. Using a `forever` loop to detect key presses is the best way to achieve smooth movements necessary for building games, but there are some problems with this method of detecting key presses, such as:

- A `forever` loop is like telling your program to run in circles as fast as it can. While it doesn't mind, this can be a waste of computer processing power that could be used for doing other things.
- Using many loops and nested blocks in your scripts can make your code difficult to read and confusing to write.
- When multiple sprites are all looping, it can make your program run slow.

For detecting occasional key presses, the `when () key pressed` block is a simpler and more effective way to code your program. The `when () key pressed` block is a hat block that waits until it detects a specific key press and then runs the blocks attached to it.

Here's how you can use the when () key pressed block to create a country line dancing program.

1. Select File ⇨ New from the top toolbar to create a new project.

2. Click the Choose Sprite from Library icon from the New Sprite: menu above the Sprite Pane.

3. Find the sprite named Boy3 Walking, click it, and click OK to add it to your project.

4. Right-click the Scratch the Cat sprite, or use the Delete tool from the top toolbar, to remove the Scratch the Cat sprite from your project.

5. Drag the when () key pressed block from the Events Block Palette and drop it in the Scripts Area.

6. Change the key in the when () key pressed block to a right arrow.

7. Drag a next costume block from the Looks Block Palette and snap it to the when () key pressed block.

8. Drag a move () steps block from the Motion Block Palette and snap it to the next costume block.

9. Drag another when () key pressed block to the Scripts Area.

   You can place this block anywhere in the Scripts Area.

10. Change the key in your new when () key pressed block to a left arrow.

11. Drag a next costume block from the Looks Block Palette and snap it to the when (left arrow) key pressed block.

12. Drag a move () steps block from the Motion Block Palette and snap it to the next costume block.

13. Change the value in the move () steps block to **–10**.

At this point, your sprite can walk back and forth. Try it out! Your Scripts Area should look like Figure 5-2.

This is a good start, but if you've ever seen country line dancers, you know that every once in a while the dancers kick their legs or slap their shoes or something similar.

Chris learned everything he knows about country line dancing by watching videos on YouTube.com. He also used to own a cowboy hat. Eva is a super-talented dancer and knows several different types of line dances. Now might be a good point to take a break, listen to some music, and practice your line dancing.

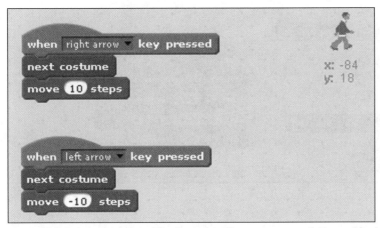

FIGURE 5-2 Forward and backward walking scripts with Event blocks

Follow these steps to make the line dancer do a kick when you press the space bar.

1. Drag another when () key pressed block to the Scripts Area.

2. Change the key in the when () key pressed block to a space.

3. Drag a switch costume to () block from the Looks Block Palette and snap it to the when (space bar) key pressed block.

4. Change the value in the switch costume to () block to **boy3-walking-c.**

5. Drag a turn counter-clockwise () degrees block from the Motion Block Palette and snap it to the switch costume to () block.

6. Change the value of the turn counter-clockwise () degrees to **30**.

7. Drag a say () for () secs block to the Scripts Area and snap it to the turn counter-clockwise () degrees block.

   Change the first value in the say () for () secs block to say **Yee Haw!** Change the number of secs to **1**.

8. Drag a turn clockwise () degrees block from the Motion Block Palette and snap it to the say (Yee Haw!) for (1) secs block.

9. Change the value of the turn clockwise block to **30** degrees.

Your Scripts Area should now look like Figure 5-3.

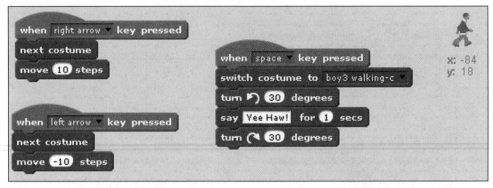

FIGURE 5-3 The line dancing scripts

DIGGING INTO THE CODE

Notice that you didn't use a `when green flag clicked` block in this project. When you begin a script with a hat block, Scratch automatically listens for the event attached to the hat blocks any time the project is open, whether you click the Green Flag or not.

Try out your project again by pressing the arrow keys and then pressing the space bar. Does the dancer move and kick and do the words "Yee Haw!" display? If so, congratulations! If not, check all your blocks carefully to make sure that everything is correct before moving on to the next steps.

If the dancer isn't responding when you press keys, you may need to click your mouse in the Stage to tell your browser to pay attention, or **focus**, on it.

When you click an item in a browser to highlight it or make it active, this is called giving that item **focus**.

In this section, you make copies of the line dancer so that he doesn't have to dance alone. Follow these steps:

1. Right-click the sprite in the Sprite Pane and select Duplicate.

   Scratch creates a copy of the Boy sprite in the Sprite Pane and on the Stage. Notice that all of the sprite's scripts are copied as well.

2. Duplicate the new sprite using the same method or by using the Duplicate button in the top toolbar.

3. Create three more copies of the sprite.

   You should now have six identical sprites in your Sprite Pane and on the Stage.

4. Click and drag the sprites in the Stage to rearrange them into two lines of three, as shown in Figure 5-4.

FIGURE 5-4 Arrange the dancers into lines

When you press the right or left arrow keys or the space bar, all the dancers should move together, just like in a real line dance.

CHALLENGE

Can you figure out how to add music to the background of the project? If you need a hint, take a look inside our script at `https://scratch.mit.edu/projects/82856436/` and click the backdrop in the Backdrop Pane to discover how we added music.

Using Backdrop Change Events

The Stage in Scratch is a special kind of sprite. Like other sprites, you can attach scripts to it. And, like other sprites, you can change the way the Stage looks. Every sprite in Scratch can have multiple different looks, or costumes. The Stage's costumes are called backdrops.

The **backdrop** is what displays behind your sprite on the Stage. A backdrop is a costume for your Stage.

The `when backdrop switches to ()` block, shown in Figure 5-5, starts a script when it detects that the backdrop on the Stage has changed to the backdrop you select.

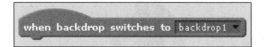

FIGURE 5-5 The `when backdrop switches to ()` block

To try out the `when backdrop switches to ()` block, make a program that plays different sounds when different backdrops display. Follow these steps to get started:

1. Select File ⇨ New from the top menu bar to create a new project.

2. Click the Choose Backdrop from Library icon from the Backdrop Pane.

   The Backdrop Library opens.

3. Find the backdrop named Space, select it, and click OK to add it to your project.

4. Click the Choose Backdrop from Library icon again.

5. Select the backdrop named Train Tracks 1 and click OK to add it to your project.

6. Click the current backdrop in the Backdrop Pane (which should be the Train Tracks 1 backdrop).

You see the Backdrop Editor, as shown in Figure 5-6.

FIGURE 5-6 The Backdrop Editor

7. Select the blank white backdrop in the Backdrop Editor. Then right-click and select Delete or use the Delete tool from the top toolbar to delete it.

8. Click the Scripts tab at the top of the Backdrop Editor to add some custom scripts to your Stage.

9. Drag the `when backdrop switches to ()` block from the Events Block Palette to the Scripts Area.

10. Make sure that Train Tracks 1 is selected inside the block, as shown in Figure 5-7.

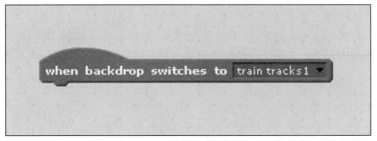

FIGURE 5-7 Select the backdrop in the `when backdrop switches to ()` block

11. Drag a `play sound () until done` block from the Sound Block Palette to the Scripts Area and snap it to the bottom of the `when backdrop switches to (train tracks1)` block.

12. Click the Sounds tab at the top of the Scripts Area to switch to the Sound Editor.

13. Click the Choose Sound from Library icon in the New Sound menu, as shown in Figure 5-8.

    The Sound Library opens.

New Sound from Library icon

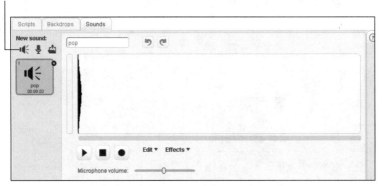

FIGURE 5-8 Click the Choose Sound from Library button

14. Find the Guitar Strum sound, click it, and click OK to add it to your project.

 Scratch doesn't have any train sounds built in (yet), but we think this guitar strum goes well with the train tracks picture.

15. Click the Scripts tab at the top of the Sound Editor to return to the Scripts Area.

16. Change the sound inside the `play sound () until done` block to the guitar strum sound.

17. Double-click the `when backdrop switches to (train tracks 1)` block to make sure that it works correctly and that the sound plays.

Next, wire up the space bar so that it causes the backdrop to change.

1. Drag a `when () key pressed` block from the Events Block Palette to the Scripts Area and place it anywhere.

2. Drag the `next backdrop` block from the Looks Block Palette to the Scripts Area and snap it to the bottom of the `when (space) key pressed` block, as shown in Figure 5-9.

FIGURE 5-9 Snap a `next backdrop` block to the `when (space) key pressed` block

Now try it out! When you press the space bar, the backdrop changes from train tracks to the space backdrop. Press the space bar again to change between the two backdrops. Listen for the guitar strum!

CHALLENGE

Try adding another sound that plays when the backdrop switches to the space backdrop.

Implementing Sensing and Timing Events

This next Event block is a fun one! It's actually more like several different Event blocks in one. It currently has three different things that it can detect and start scripts with video motion, loudness, and timing.

This three-in-one Event block is called the when () > () block, and it's shown in Figure 5-10.

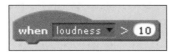

FIGURE 5-10 The when () > () block

Detecting Video Motion

If you have a camera attached to your computer, or built into it, you can tell Scratch to watch for movement in front of the camera. The when (video motion) > () block detects if the amount of motion exceeds the amount you set as the value of the block. If so, Scratch runs the scripts attached to the when (video motion) > () block.

The highest possible value for the when (video motion) > () block is 100.

Measuring Loudness

If you have a microphone on your computer, you can use loudness to detect how much sound the microphone is picking up. If it's louder than the amount you specify, the blocks attached to the when (loudness) > () block run.

The highest possible value for the when (loudness) > () block is 100.

Waiting for the Right Time

The when (timer) > () block watches the value of the timer. When it's greater than the number you specify, the blocks attached to it run.

Getting Your Message Across

The next three Event blocks have to do with messages and **broadcasting**. Broadcasting is the way that sprites can talk to each other. Here's how it works:

1. One sprite broadcasts a message, which is like a radio station's broadcast.

2. If another sprite is listening for a particular message, that sprite can hear it and do something in response.

3. If no other sprite is listening for a particular broadcasted message, the message won't cause any action to happen.

Broadcasting in Scratch works like a secret message that only sprites can tune into and hear.

Broadcasting is useful everywhere in Scratch, but it's particularly important for games and for animations where sprites need to take action in response to things that other sprites do. In a basketball video game, for example, you might have the crowd cheer when a player scores. To program this in Scratch, you would have the basketball broadcast a message when it goes through the hoop. The crowd then can listen for this broadcasting message and cheer whenever it happens.

The broadcasting blocks are shown in Figure 5-11.

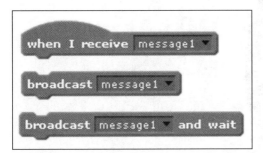

FIGURE 5-11 The broadcasting blocks

The three broadcasting blocks do the following:

- The `when I receive ()` block is a hat block that listens for a message and starts a script when it detects that message.

- The `broadcast ()` block sends out a message that you can make other sprites listen for and respond to.

- The `broadcast () and wait` block sends out a message and stops running a script until the message is received and the script attached to the receiving block finishes running. For example, you might have a game where a character touching a door handle sends a message that triggers a door opening animation. By using `broadcast () and wait` you can make sure that the door animation finishes (and the door is open all the way) before the character tries to go through the door.

To see how broadcasting works, create a script that makes two sprites have a dance-off.

1. Select File ➪ New from the top toolbar to create a new project.

2. Right-click Scratch the Cat in the Sprite Pane and select Delete, or use the Delete tool from the top toolbar.

3. Use the Choose Sprite from Library icon to open the library and add the CM Hip-Hop sprite to your project.

4. Use the Choose Sprite from Library icon to open the library and add the D-Money Hip-Hop sprite to your project.

5. Arrange the two sprites so that they're standing next to each other.

   Your Stage and Sprite Pane should now look similar to Figure 5-12.

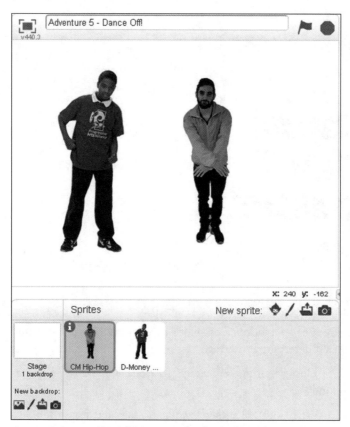

FIGURE 5-12 Two dancers on the Stage

6. Select the CM Hip-Hop sprite in the Sprites Pane.

7. Drag a `when green flag clicked` block from the Events Block Palette to the Scripts Area.

8. Drag a `broadcast ()` block from the Events Block Palette and snap it to the bottom of the `when green flag clicked` block.

9. Click the drop-down menu in the `broadcast ()` block and select New Message, as shown in Figure 5-13.

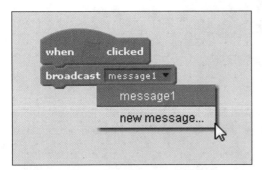

FIGURE 5-13 Create a new message

10. When the New Message dialog box appears, type the words **Dance off!** into it.

11. Drag a `when I receive ()` block from the Events Block Palette to the Stage and drop it anywhere.

12. Click the drop-down menu in the `when I receive ()` block and select Dance Off!

    This is the event that triggers the CM Hip-Hop sprite to start dancing.

13. Drag a `repeat ()` block from the Control Block Palette and snap it to the bottom of the `when I receive ()` block.

    If it's not already, set the value of this block to **10**.

14. Drag a `next costume` block from the Looks Block Palette and snap it inside the `repeat (10)` block.

15. Drag a `wait ()` secs block from the Control Block Palette and snap it onto the bottom of the `next costume` block.

16. Change the value of the `wait ()` secs block to **.1**.

17. Drag a `broadcast ()` block from the Events Block Palette and snap it to the bottom of the `repeat (10)` block.

18. Select New Message from the drop-down menu and create a new message that says **Your turn!**

Your Scripts Area should now look like Figure 5-14.

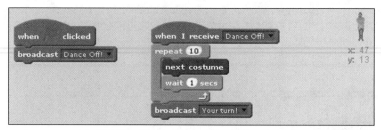

FIGURE 5-14 CM Hip-Hop's dancing scripts

When this sprite finishes his dance loop and broadcasts "Your turn!" that's the cue for the other sprite to start his dance. Follow these steps to make the other sprite listen for his turn and start dancing.

1. Click the D-Money Hip-Hop sprite in the Sprite Pane.

The blank D-Money Scripts Area displays.

2. Drag a `when I receive ()` block from the Events Block Palette to the Scripts Area.

3. Select Your turn! from the drop-down menu.

4. Drag a `repeat ()` block from the Control Block Palette to the Scripts Area and snap it to the `when I receive ()` block.

Set the value in the `repeat ()` block to **10**.

5. Drag a `next costume` block from the Looks Block Palette and snap it inside of the `repeat (10)` block.

6. Drag a `wait () secs` block from the Control Block Palette and snap it to the bottom of the `next costume` block.

7. Change the value of the `wait () secs` block to **.1**.

8. Drag a `broadcast ()` block from the Events Block Palette and snap it to the bottom of the `repeat (10)` block. Change its value to **Dance Off!**

When you're done, the Scripts Area for the D-Money Hip-Hop sprite should look like Figure 5-15.

That's all there is to it! When you're ready, click the Green Flag to watch the dance off!

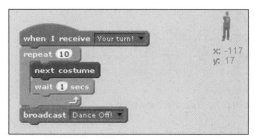

FIGURE 5-15 The finished D-Money Hip-Hop script

Putting on the Big Event

Using event and broadcasting blocks, you can put together really amazing projects that use multiple sprites, backdrops, and timing to have all sorts of fun. And, what's more fun than a ballerina, a dinosaur, and a talking cat all in the same place?

In this adventure, you use everything you've learned about events to put on a three-ring circus. Let's get started!

Figure 5-16 shows what the Stage will look like when you click the Green Flag for this project.

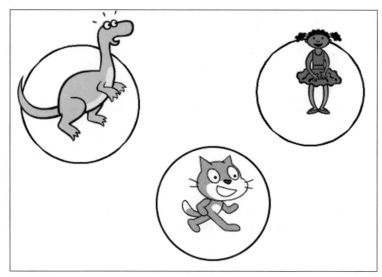

FIGURE 5-16 The three-ring circus project

In addition to the screen shown in Figure 5-16, you will also create three separate scenes for each of the sprites where they will show off their unique talents.

Setting the Stages

To get started building the three-ring circus, you need to find all the sprites and backdrops that the circus will use and add them to the project. Follow these steps to start building the Scratch circus.

1. Select File ⇨ New from the top toolbar to create a new project.

2. Click Choose Sprite from Library from the New Sprite menu.

3. Locate the sprite named Dinosaur1 and add it to your project.

4. Click Choose Sprite from Library and add the Ballerina sprite to your project.

5. Click Paint New Backdrop from the Backdrop Pane.

   The Backdrop Editor opens.

6. Select any color from the Color Palette to use for the three rings of your circus.

7. Click the Ellipse tool in the Paint Editor.

8. While holding down the Shift key, drag the Ellipse tool to draw a circle in the Paint Editor.

   Notice that right after you draw the circle, it has a box around it and small circle in the middle. You can use this to adjust the size and position of your circle.

9. After you have your circle positioned, click your mouse on the Stage outside of where you drew the circle.

10. Use the Ellipse tool to draw two more circles and position them similarly to the circles in Figure 5-16.

If you make a mistake, use the Eraser tool to remove part of your three rings, or use the Clear button at the top of the Paint Editor to erase everything and start over.

11. Click the backdrop name box in the upper-left corner of the Paint Editor and change the name of your backdrop to **three rings**, as shown in Figure 5-17.

12. Click Choose Backdrop from Library from the New Backdrop menu.

13. Locate the backdrop named Stage1 and add it to your project.

    This is the backdrop for the Scratch the Cat show.

14. Click Choose Backdrop from Library from the New Backdrop menu.

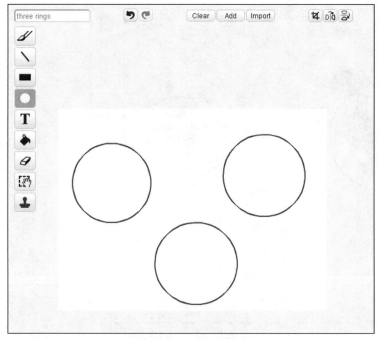

FIGURE 5-17 Naming the three-ring backdrop

15. Locate the backdrop named Castle3 and add it to your project.

    This is the backdrop for the dinosaur's show.

The Scratch Backdrop Library is in alphabetical order to make it easier to find the backdrop you're searching for.

16. Click Choose Backdrop from Library from the New Backdrop menu.

17. Locate the backdrop named Spotlight-Stage and add it to your project.

    This is the backdrop for the ballerina's show.

18. Select the scissors (Delete tool) from the top toolbar and use it to remove the blank white backdrop from your project, or click the *x* in a circle in the upper-right corner of the thumbnail image for the blank white backdrop to delete it.

19. Select the three rings backdrop in the backdrop pane so it shows up on the Stage. Drag the sprites around the screen to position them inside of each ring, as shown in Figure 5-18.

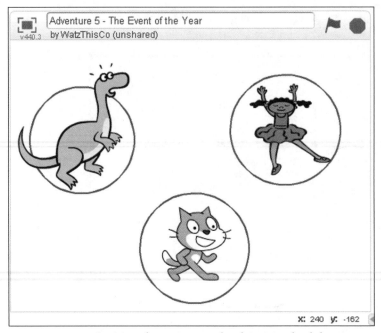

FIGURE 5-18 Position the sprites on the three-ring backdrop

Now that you've added the sprites and backdrops that you need for this project, you're ready to move on and start writing the scripts to make this circus go!

Programming the Ringleader

The circus program will feature three different performances from the three different sprites. You'll be able to see each performance by clicking one of the three performers. Two of the performers are hidden while the selected sprite performs his or her special show. Each performer also has his or her own particular backdrop.

Scratch the Cat will be the ringleader of the circus. To program her performance, follow these steps.

1. Click Scratch the Cat in the Sprite Pane, and select the Scripts tab to view the Scripts Area.

2. Drag a `when this sprite clicked` block from the Events Block Palette to the Scripts Area.

3. Drag a `broadcast ()` block from the Events Block Palette and snap it to the `when this sprite clicked` block.

4. Select New Message from the `broadcast ()` block's drop-down menu.

5. Create a new message that says **Ringleader Show**.

6. Drag a `glide () secs to x: () y: ()` to the Scripts Area and snap it to the bottom of the `broadcast (Ringleader Show)` block.

   Change the `x:` value to **–76** and the `y:` value to **–80**.

7. Drag a `say () for () secs` block to the Scripts Area and snap it to the `glide () secs to x: () y: ()` block.

8. Change the value of the `say () for () secs` to **Welcome to the big show!**

9. Drag a `play sound ()` block to the Scripts Area and snap it to the bottom of the `say (Welcome to the show!) for () secs` block.

10. Select the Sounds tab at the top of the Scripts Area to open the Sound Editor.

11. Click the Choose New Sound from Library icon in the New Sound menu.

12. Locate the sound named Clapping and add it to your project.

13. Click the Scripts tab to switch back to the Scripts Area.

14. Change the value of the `play sound ()` block to clapping.

15. Drag a `wait () secs` block from the Control Block Palette and snap it to the bottom of the `play sound ()` block.

16. Drag a `broadcast ()` block from the Events Block Palette and snap it to the `wait () secs` block.

17. Select New Message from the drop-down menu in the `broadcast ()` block and make the new message say **Three Rings**.

   The Script Area for Scratch the Cat should now look similar to Figure 5-19.

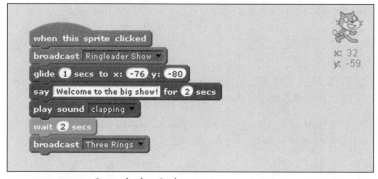

FIGURE 5-19 Scratch the Cat's script

Programming the Ballerina Show

Most of the code for the ballerina is the same as the code for the ringleader, so you can save some time and steps by making an exact copy of Scratch the Cat's script. You add it to the ballerina and then customize it. Follow these steps.

1. With Scratch the Cat selected in the Sprite Pane, click the `when this sprite clicked` block in the Scripts Area and drag the entire script so that it's hovering over the Ballerina sprite in the Sprite Pane. Then let go of your mouse button.

2. Click the ballerina in the Sprite Pane. You should now see an exact copy of Scratch the Cat's script in the ballerina's Scripts Area.

3. Click the drop-down menu in the `broadcast ()` block and create a new message that says **Ballet Show**.

4. Click the `say () for () secs` block and drag it down to disconnect it from the `glide () secs to x: () y: ()` block, as shown in Figure 5-20.

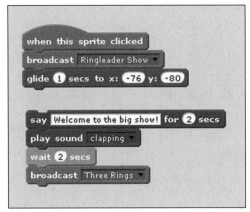

FIGURE 5-20 Disconnecting the `say () for () secs` block from the `glide ()` block

5. Click the `play sound ()` block and drag it down to separate it from the `say () for () secs` block, as shown in Figure 5-21.

6. Click and drag the `say () for () secs` block back to the Block Palette to remove it from the Scripts Area.

7. Drag a `repeat ()` block from the Control Block Palette to the Scripts Area and snap it to the bottom of the `glide () secs to x: () y: ()` block.

   Change the `x:` value to **26** and the `y:` value to **0**.

8. Change the value in the `repeat ()` block to **12**.

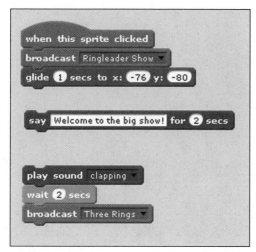

FIGURE 5-21 Disconnecting the `play sound ()` block from the `say () for ()` secs block

9. Drag a `next costume` block from the Looks Block Palette to the Scripts Area and snap it inside the `repeat ()` block.

DIGGING INTO THE CODE

You repeat the `next costume` block 12 times because the ballerina has four different costumes. Repeating 12 times causes her to do each of her dance moves three times and then end up where she started.

10. Drag a `wait () secs` block from the Control Blocks Palette and snap it to the bottom of the `next costume` block.

11. Change the value of the `wait () secs` block to **0.5**.

12. Drag the `play sound ()` block that is already in the Scripts Area, along with the blocks attached to it, and snap them onto the bottom of the `repeat ()` block.

13. Click the drop-down menu in the `broadcast ()` block at the end of the ballerina's script and make sure that it's set to Three Rings.

This completes the ballerina's script! Your Scripts Area for the ballerina should look like Figure 5-22.

FIGURE 5-22 The finished ballerina script

Move on to the next section to create the dinosaur's script.

VIDEO

To watch Chris script the Dino Show, visit the companion website at www.wiley.com/go/adventuresincoding and select Adventure 5!

Programming the Dinosaur Show

Here's how to write the script for the dinosaur's show.

1. With the ballerina selected in the Sprite Pane, drag the script and drop it onto the Dinosaur sprite in the Sprite Pane.

2. Select the Dinosaur sprite in the Sprite Pane.

   The dinosaur's Scripts Area opens with an exact copy of the ballerina's script.

3. Click the drop-down menu in the first `broadcast ()` block to New Message and create a new message that says **Dino Show**.

   Change the x: value to **0** and the y: to **–50**.

4. Change the value in the `repeat ()` block to **14**.

DIGGING INTO THE CODE

Because the dinosaur has seven different costumes, changing the value in the `repeat()` block to 14 makes sure that the dinosaur goes through his costumes twice and then always finishes with the same costume he started in.

That's it for the dinosaur for now! When you're done, the dinosaur's Scripts Area should look like Figure 5-23.

FIGURE 5-23 The dinosaur's script

Programming the Stage

Now that you've programmed the performances for each sprite, it's time to create the scripts that change the backdrops to match the performances.

Follow these steps to create the scripts that change the backdrops when different messages and events happen.

1. Click the Stage sprite in the lower-left corner of the Scratch Project Editor.

2. Drag a `when green flag clicked` block to the Scripts Area.

3. Drag a `switch backdrop to ()` block from the Looks Block Palette and snap it to the `when green flag clicked` block.

4. Set the drop-down menu in this `switch backdrop to ()` block to Three Rings.

5. Drag a `when I receive ()` block from the Events Block Palette to the Scripts Area.

6. Change the value in the drop-down menu for this block to Ringleader Show.

7. Drag a `switch backdrop to ()` block from the Looks Block Palette to the Scripts Area and connect it to the `when I receive ()` block.

8. Select stage1 from the drop-down menu for this `when I receive ()` block.

   You should now have two scripts in the Stage's Scripts Area, as shown in Figure 5-24.

FIGURE 5-24 The first two Stage scripts

9. Right-click the script that starts with `when I receive ()` and select Duplicate.

10. Change the value in the duplicate `when I receive ()` block to Ballet Show.

11. Change the value of the switch `backdrop to ()` block to Spotlight-stage.

12. Right-click the duplicated script and make a copy of it by selecting Duplicate.

13. Change the value of the `when I receive ()` block in this new copy to Dino Show.

14. Change the value of the switch `backdrop to ()` block to Castle3.

15. Make one more copy of this script.

16. Change the value of the `when I receive ()` block to Three Rings.

17. Change the value of the `switch backdrop to ()` block to Three Rings.

    You should now have five scripts in your Stage's Scripts Area, as shown in Figure 5-25.

FIGURE 5-25 The finished Stage scripts

DIGGING INTO THE CODE

Each of these hat blocks is set to listen for a message broadcasted from a sprite and then display the appropriate backdrop.

Showing and Hiding Sprites

The last step in programming the three-ring circus is to program the showing and hiding of the sprites when different performers are clicked.

1. Click Scratch the Cat and position her inside of the circle on the Stage.

2. Drag a when green flag clicked block to the Scripts Area.

3. Drag a show block from the Looks Block Palette and snap it to the when green flag clicked block.

4. Drag a go to x: () y: () block from the Motion Block Palette and snap it to the show block.

   It should already have values in it for the current location of Scratch the Cat.

5. Drag three when I receive () blocks from the Events Block Palette to the Scripts Area.

6. Set one of the when I receive () blocks to Dino Show, one to Ballet Show, and one to Three Rings.

7. Drag two `hide` blocks from the Looks Block Palette. Snap one of them onto the `when I receive (Dino Show)` and one to the `when I receive (Ballet Show)` block.

8. Drag a `show` block from the Looks Block Palette and snap it to the `when I receive (Three Rings)` block.

9. Drag a `go to x: () y: ()` block from the Motion Block Palette and snap it to the bottom of the `show` block attached to the `when I receive (Three Rings)` block.

    Your Scripts Area for Scratch the Cat should now look something like Figure 5-26.

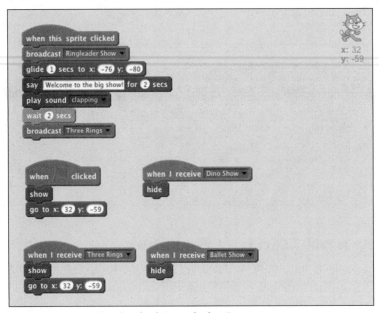

FIGURE 5-26 The finished Scratch the Cat scripts

10. Now repeat Steps 2 through 7 for each of the other two sprites. Make sure to use a `show` block instead of the `hide` block for the code that is associated with the sprite you are working on.

If you choose to duplicate the scripts from Scratch the Cat's Script Area and add them to your other sprites, be sure to reset the values in your `go to x: () y: ()` blocks to the correct coordinates of that sprite's position on the Stage.

When you're done, the Scripts Area for the dinosaur should look similar to Figure 5-27.

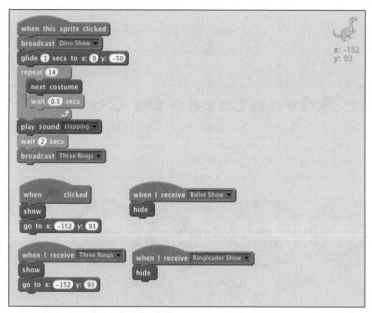

FIGURE 5-27 The finished dinosaur scripts

The Scripts Area for the ballerina should look like Figure 5-28.

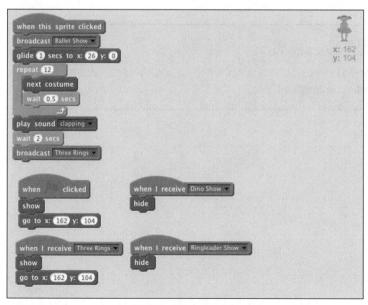

FIGURE 5-28 The finished ballerina scripts

Congratulations! You've done it! That was the biggest project you've built so far. Click the Green Flag and try it out. Click any sprite, watch it do its thing and when it's done, return to the three-ring circus view.

Pat yourself on the back and give out a mighty roar of celebration! If your program is not running quite right, go back over the steps and check your work carefully.

Further Adventures in Coding

David J. Malan created a fun tutorial about events in which you can learn how he created the game called Oscartime. Visit `http://cs.harvard.edu/malan/scratch/events.php` to try it out!

Achievement Unlocked: **The Main Event**

In the Next Adventure

The next adventure shows you how you can write code to store and remember facts and information in Scratch!

Adventure 6
Variables and Lists

WHEN YOU LEARN an interesting fact about birds or the name of a new friend, you store it in your memory. In the same way, when a computer keeps track of your score in a game or remembers your name, it's using computer memory.

In your head, you remember facts and figures by giving them names. Without a name, any fact or figure is useless. For example, the number 15,000 is just a number. But with a name, it becomes an interesting thing to remember, for example:

Elephants can weigh as much as 15,000 pounds!

Computers remember things in the same way as you do. In programming languages, the name that's given to something you want the computer to remember is called a **variable**.

> A **variable** is a box that you can give a name to. This name will stand for all the data inside of that box.

DEFINITIONS

In this adventure, you find out how to use variables in Scratch to remember and keep track of things.

Understanding Variable Blocks

Variables are like boxes into which you can put any combination of words, numbers, dates, or other values that you want to use or remember in your program.

If you want to write a program that asks a user to input the answers to several questions, you can use the `ask () and wait` block that you learned about in Adventure 4. After each question is asked, the answer is placed into the `answer` block.

Follow these steps to create a simple quiz program:

1. Select File ⇨ New from the top toolbar to create a new project.

2. Drag the `ask () and wait` block from the Sensing Block Palette to the Scripts Area.

   Leave the question in the `ask () and wait` block set to "What's your name?".

3. Drag a `think () for () secs` block from the Looks Block Palette and snap it to the bottom of the `ask () and wait` block.

4. Drag an `answer` block from the Sensing Block Palette and snap it inside of the `think () for () secs` block.

Your Scripts Area should now look like Figure 6-1.

FIGURE 6-1 Asking a question and thinking the answer

People say that the best way to remember people's names when you first meet them is to say their name right away. This is exactly what Scratch the Cat is trying to do in this program.

Double-click the `ask () and wait` block to run the program. When Scratch the Cat asks for your name, type it in and press Enter on your keyboard, or click the checkbox on the Stage. Scratch the Cat "thinks" your name, as shown in Figure 6-2.

Let's see what happens when Scratch the Cat asks another question. Follow these steps:

1. Right-click the `ask () and wait` block in your Scripts Area and select Duplicate.

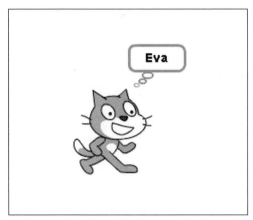

FIGURE 6-2 Scratch the Cat is thinking about your name

A copy of the connected `ask ()  and wait` and `think  (answer)  for  ()  secs` block is created.

2. Connect the duplicated blocks to the original two blocks.

   Your Scripts Area should now look like Figure 6-3.

FIGURE 6-3 Asking and thinking about two names

3. Double-click the first `ask ()  and wait` block.

4. Answer the first question with your own name.

   Scratch the Cat "thinks" about your name, just as before.

5. Answer the second question with someone else's name.

   Scratch the Cat "thinks" about that new name.

Scratch the Cat is able to ask a question and then repeat your answer. But, as soon as she asks another question, she forgets the answer to the first one. That must be so embarrassing for her at parties!

We can solve this problem and help Scratch the Cat to be a better party host by using variables.

Variables Have Names

In this section, you create two variables to remember the two different answers to Scratch the Cat's questions. Each variable in a program has a unique name that's used to remember and recall its value.

You can name variables anything you want in Scratch. For this project, you create two variables and call them Name1 and Name2.

Follow these steps to create the two variables and use them to hold the two different answers:

1. Click the Data category in the Block Palette.

   You see two buttons, Make a Variable and Make a List, as shown in Figure 6-4.

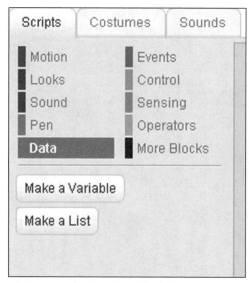

FIGURE 6-4 The Data Block Palette

2. Click Make a Variable.

   The New Variable pop-up window opens, as shown in Figure 6-5.

3. Type **Name1** into the text area to the right of Variable Name in the New Variable pop-up window.

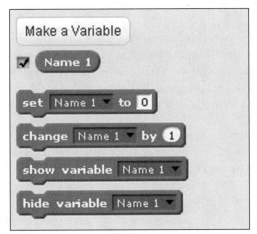

New Variable

Variable name: [   ]

● For all sprites   ○ For this sprite only

☐ Cloud variable (stored on server)

[OK] [Cancel]

FIGURE 6-5 The New Variable pop-up window

The Cloud Variable box appears only if you're signed into your Scratch account.

4. Leave everything else set as it is in the pop-up window and click OK.

   As soon as you click OK, a new block named Name1 appears in the Data Block Palette, and four new stack blocks become visible, as shown in Figure 6-6.

Make a Variable

☑ Name 1

set Name 1 ▼ to 0

change Name 1 ▼ by 1

show variable Name 1 ▼

hide variable Name 1 ▼

FIGURE 6-6 Your first variable, and the Data stack blocks

Variables Can Display on the Stage

Look at the Stage now. You see a new box in the upper-left corner with the name of your new variable and an orange box with a 0 in it, as shown in Figure 6-7. The 0 is the current value that's stored in your variable. All variables start out with a 0 in them when they're created.

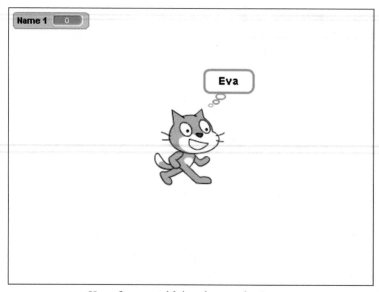

FIGURE 6-7 Your first variable's value on the Stage

When you first create a variable, it displays on the Stage. You can use a variable's display for showing the current score in a game, for example, or just to help you visualize what's happening in your program. You can drag the variable anywhere you want it to be on the Stage, or you can choose not to display it at all. To hide a variable, uncheck the checkbox next to it in the Data Block Palette, as shown in Figure 6-8.

In a moment, you'll use this Name1 variable to remember the first name that you tell Scratch the Cat. But first, use the following steps to create another variable that you'll use to help Scratch the Cat remember the second name:

1. Click the Make a Variable button in the Data Block Palette.

   The New Variable pop-up window opens.

2. Give this new variable a name of **Name2**.

3. Click OK to create the new variable.

   Your Data Blocks Palette should now look like Figure 6-9.

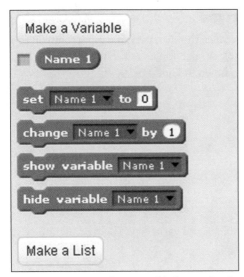

FIGURE 6-8 Hide a variable by unchecking the box next to it

For now, leave the checkboxes next to both variables checked. Variables work the same way whether you display them or not, but showing them on the Stage makes it easier for you to see what's going on in your program while you're writing it. You can hide them later on if you want!

FIGURE 6-9 The Data Block Palette with two variables

Variables Can Change

The reason variables are named *variable* is because they can vary, meaning that you can *change* the value stored inside of them. The block that you use to change the value of a variable is the set () to () stack block, shown in Figure 6-10.

FIGURE 6-10 The set () to () block

In this section, you use the set () to () block and variables to help Scratch the Cat remember two names. Follow these steps:

1. Drag a set () to () block from the Data Block Palette to the Scripts Area and snap it to the bottom of the first ask () and wait block.

2. Change the value in the set () to () block's drop-down menu to **Name1**.

3. Drag an answer block from the Sensing Block Palette and snap it into the square inside the set () to () block.

4. Drag the answer block out of the first think () block and remove it from the Scripts Area by dropping it back into the Blocks Palette.

5. Drag the Name1 variable block from the Data Block Palette and snap it inside the first think () block.

    Your Scripts Area should now look like Figure 6-11.

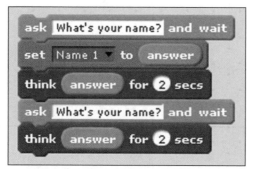

FIGURE 6-11 Storing the first answer in a variable

6. Drag another `set () to ()` block from the Data Block Palette and snap it to the bottom of the second `ask () and wait` block.

7. Change the value in this new `set () to ()` block's drop-down menu to **Name2** (if it isn't already set to that).

8. Drag an `answer` block from the Sensing Block Palette and snap it inside the `set () to ()` block.

9. Remove the `answer` block from the second `think () for () secs` block and replace it with the `Name2` variable block from the Data Block Palette.

Your Scripts Area should now look like Figure 6-12.

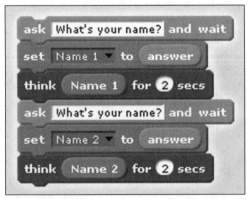

FIGURE 6-12 Storing two answers in two variables

10. Drag a `say () for () secs` block from the Looks Block Palette and snap it to the bottom of your script.

11. Drag a `join () ()` block from the Operators Block Palette and snap it into the first space in the `say () for () secs` block, as shown in Figure 6-13.

12. Drag the `Name1` variable block from the Data Block Palette and drop it into the second rectangle inside the `join () ()` block, as shown in Figure 6-14.

13. Drag another `say () for () secs` block from the Looks Block Palette and snap it to the bottom of the first one.

14. Drag a `join () ()` block from the Operators Block Palette and snap it inside the `say () for () secs` block.

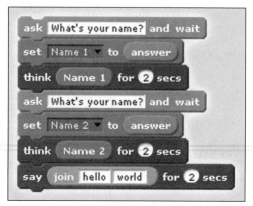

FIGURE 6-13 Snapping a join () () block inside the say () for () secs block

FIGURE 6-14 Dropping a variable block into a join () () block

15. Drag the Name2 block from the Data Block Palette and snap it inside the second space in the join () () block.

    Your Scripts Area should now look like Figure 6-15.

16. Double-click the first block in your script to run the program.

    Scratch asks you for two names and then greets you using both names!

Scratch Variables Are Persistent

Try running this script a few more times, using different names each time. Notice that after you submit a new name, it replaces the name that was previously in each variable, as you can see by watching the variable boxes displayed on the Stage.

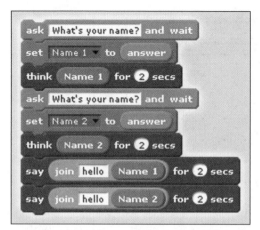

FIGURE 6-15 Remembering and saying two names

One interesting thing about variables in Scratch is that they're persistent. What this means is that you can stop a program and start it again and the program's variables will be the same as they were when you stopped the program.

You can even close the browser window or shut down your computer and return to your program later on to find that the variables will be exactly the same as they were when you left.

Scratch Variables Are Big

If variables are like boxes, Scratch has some very big boxes.

Try entering multiple names or words in response to each question Scratch the Cat asks you. It doesn't matter what you type, the variable remembers it until you run the program again and change the variable's value.

Figure 6-16 shows how you can enter quite a bit of text into the `ask () and wait` text box and Scratch stores it the same as when you enter just a single name.

You can store up to 10,240 characters in a single Scratch variable. That's about the same as the number of characters between the beginning of this adventure and this point! So, Scratch the Cat can remember even the longest names that anyone tells her.

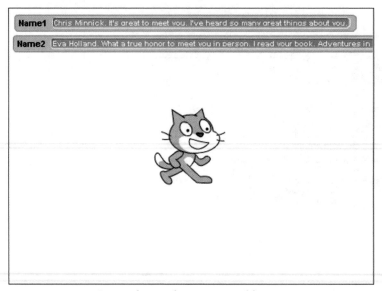

FIGURE 6-16 Storing long values in a variable

Making Lists

You've seen how you can use variables to store single values in Scratch. But, what if you have a long list of names to remember? Creating all those variables to store names can be time consuming! And, what if you don't know how many names you want Scratch the Cat to remember?

This is where lists come in! Lists in Scratch are just like lists in real life. You can add items to them, remove items from them, and change any item from one value to another.

This section shows you how to use lists with loops to make Scratch the Cat ask for and remember as many names as you'd like!

Making a List

Lists work just like variables, except each list can hold more than one value. In other programming languages, lists are called **arrays**.

An **array** is a special kind of variable that can hold multiple values using the same name.

Follow these steps to create your first list in Scratch.

1. Select File ➪ New from the top toolbar.

2. Click Make a List in the Data Block Palette.

   The New List pop-up window opens, as shown in Figure 6-17.

FIGURE 6-17 The New List pop-up window

3. Enter Names in the List name text box and click OK.

   The Names list appears in the Data Block Palette, along with the nine list blocks, as shown in Figure 6-18.

FIGURE 6-18 The List blocks

Take a look at the Stage. The Names list is displayed in the top-left corner, as shown in Figure 6-19.

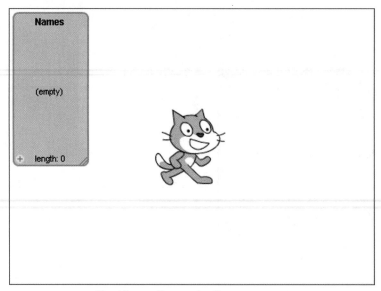

FIGURE 6-19 The Names list on the Stage

When a new list is created, it doesn't have any values in it. A list with nothing in it is called an empty list. Follow these steps to add and remove a couple of items from your list.

1. Click the small plus sign in the lower-left corner of the Names list on the Stage.

   A blank text area appears at the top of the list and the length of the list changes to 1, as shown in Figure 6-20.

2. Enter a name into the blank text box in the Names list.

   If you press Enter (or Return) now, a new blank item is added to the list. If you click anywhere outside of the list, the value you entered is stored without creating a new, blank item.

3. Add several more items to the list.

4. Click inside each of the list items and click the x with a circle around it (see Figure 6-21) to delete each of them.

Most of the time when you use lists, you add and remove items from them using Scripts that you create. In the next section, you find out how to use the List stack blocks to make Scratch the Cat remember a bunch of names!

FIGURE 6-20 Adding an item to a list

FIGURE 6-21 Deleting items from a list in the Stage

The Ultimate Party Host

In this project, you create a program that can be very helpful at parties, in school, and just about anywhere where a lot of people gather. The ultimate party host can remember any number of peoples' names, in order, along with each person's age.

Introducing the Lists and Variables

The first thing you do is create the arrays and a variable that the program needs.

1. Click File ⇨ New to create a new project.

2. In the Data Block Palette, create two new lists: **Names** and **Ages**.

3. Create a new variable called **Name Number**.

4. Your Data Block Palette should now look like Figure 6-22.

FIGURE 6-22 The Party Host's variable and lists

5. Drag a when green flag clicked block from the Events Block Palette to the Scripts Area.

Asking for Names and Ages

Next, you use a question and a loop to gather information about each party guest. Follow these steps:

1. Drag the ask () and wait block from the Sensing Block Palette and change its question to **How many people are there?**

2. Drag a repeat () block from the Control Block Palette and snap it to the bottom of the ask () and wait block.

3. Drag an `answer` block from the Sensing Block Palette and drop it inside the oval space in the `repeat ()` block.

4. Drag an `ask () and wait` block from the Sensing Block Palette and snap it inside the `repeat` block.

Remember that the C-blocks such as the `repeat ()` block create loops.

Leave the question in the `ask () and wait` block set to "What's your name?"

5. Drag an `add () to ()` block from the Data Block Palette and snap it to the bottom of the `ask () and wait` block inside the `repeat ()` block.

6. Drag an `answer` block from the Sensing Block Palette and snap it inside the `add () to ()` block.

7. Using the drop-down menu, change the second value in the `add (answer) to ()` block to **Names**.

Your Scripts Area should now look like Figure 6-23.

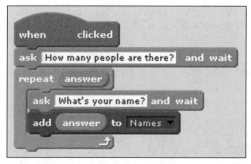

FIGURE 6-23 Gathering names and adding them to a list

8. Drag an `ask () and wait` block from the Sensing Block Palette to the Scripts Area and snap it to the `add (answer) to (Names)` block inside the `repeat ()` block.

9. Change the question in this block to **How old are you?**

10. Drag an `add () to ()` block from the Data Block Palette to the Scripts Area and snap it to the bottom of the `ask (How old are you?) and wait` block.

11. Drag an `answer` block from the Sensing Block Palette and place it inside the `add () to ()` block.

12. Change the drop-down menu in the `add (answer) to ()` block to **Ages**.

Your Scripts Area should now look like Figure 6-24.

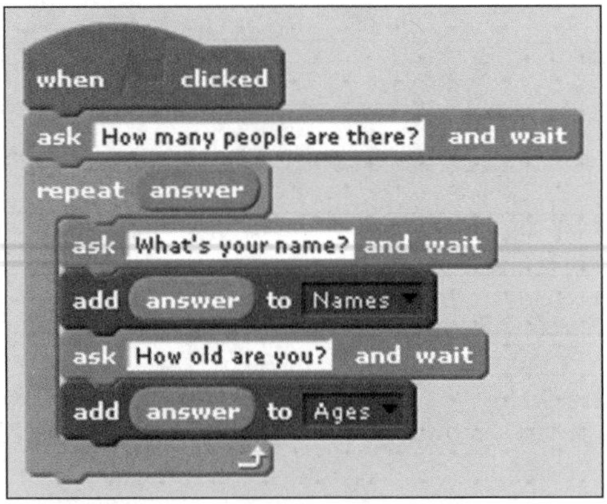

![Scratch script showing: when clicked, ask How many people are there? and wait, repeat answer, ask What's your name? and wait, add answer to Names, ask How old are you? and wait, add answer to Ages]

FIGURE 6-24 Adding to the Names and Ages lists

Click the Green Flag to try out your program! Enter a number in response to the first question. Keep the number pretty low for now (two or three) so that it doesn't take too long to answer all the questions.

As you answer the questions, items are added to the two lists on the Stage. In the next part, you write code to make Scratch remember and repeat the names and ages of each person.

Recalling Names and Ages

To remember and use items in a list after you've created it, you put the number of a list item into the `item () of ()` block. If you want to make a sprite say what the third item in the Names list is, for example, you'd use the block shown in Figure 6-25.

FIGURE 6-25 Saying the third item in the Names list

In this adventure, the program you create first tells you how many items are in the list of partygoers and then it says the names and ages of each guest. To do this, you use a loop to repeat the say () for () secs block for each item in the list. Here's how you do it:

1. Drag a say () for () secs block and snap it to the bottom of the repeat () block.

2. Drag a join () () block from the Operators Block Palette and snap it into the first space in the say () for () secs block.

3. Drag another join () () block from the Operators Block Palette and snap it into the first space in the join () () block you just placed.

4. Change the first value in this new join () () block to **I know**.

5. Drag a length of () block from the Data Block Palette and snap it inside of the second space in this join () () block.

6. Change the value in the length of (Names) block to **Names**.

7. Change the value in the second space in the outer join () () block to **people**.

   When this whole block is done, it should look like Figure 6-26.

FIGURE 6-26 The finished people counting block

8. Drag a set () to () block from the Data Block Palette and snap it to the bottom of the say () for () secs block.

9. Change the first value of the set () to () block to **Name Number** and change the second value to **0**.

10. Drag a repeat () block from the Control Block Palette and snap it to the end of the script.

11. Drag a length of () block from the Data Block Palette and drop it inside the oval in the repeat () block.

12. Change the value in the length of () block to **Names**.

    At this point, the repeat () loop runs one time for each item in the list called Names.

13. Drag a change () to () block from the Data Block Palette to inside of the repeat (length of (Names)) block.

14. Change the first value in the `change () to ()` block to **Name Number** and the second value to **1**.

15. Drag a `say () for () secs` block to the Scripts Area and snap it inside the `repeat (length of (Names))` block, after the `change (Name Number by (1))` block.

16. Drag a `join () ()` block and snap it inside of the first space in the `say () for () secs` block.

17. Drag an `item () of ()` block from the Data Block Palette and snap it into the first value in the `join () ()` block.

18. Drag the `Name Number` variable block into the first value of the `item () of ()` block and set the second value to **Names**.

19. Drag an `item () of ()` block into the second value in the `join () ()` block.

20. Drag a `Name Number` variable block into the first value of this new `item () of ()` block and set the second value to **Names**.

21. Drag another `join () ()` block into the second open value of the first `join () ()` block. In the first open space, type the word **is** with spaces before and after it.

22. Drag an `item () of ()` block from the Data Block Palette into the second value in the `join () ()` block.

23. Drag a `Name Number` variable block into the first value of this new `item () of ()` block and set the second value to **Ages**.

   You may need to take apart blocks and put them back together in order to get it just right. Compare your finished `say () for () secs` block to the finished version in Figure 6-27.

FIGURE 6-27 The finished `say () for ()` block to remember names and ages

24. Drag a `delete () of ()` block from the Data Block Palette to the bottom of the `when green flag clicked` block.

25. Change the first value of the `delete () of ()` block to **all**, and change the second value to **Ages**.

26. Drag another `delete () of ()` block from the Data Block Palette and snap it to the bottom of the first `delete () of ()` block.

27. Change the first value of this `delete () of ()` block to **all**, and change the second value to **Names**.

When your program is finished, it should look like Figure 6-28.

```
when      clicked
delete  all▼ of  Ages ▼
delete  all▼ of  Names ▼
ask  How many people are there?  and wait
repeat  answer
    ask  What's your name?  and wait
    add  answer  to  Names ▼
    ask  How old are you?  and wait
    add  answer  to  Ages ▼

say  join  join  I know  length of  Names ▼   people  for  2  secs
set  Name Number ▼  to  0
repeat  length of  Names ▼
    change  Name Number ▼  by  1
    say  join  item  Name Number  of  Names ▼   join  is  item  Name Number  of  Ages ▼   for  2  secs
```

FIGURE 6-28 The finished Party Host Scratch program

How did you do? Click the Green Flag to run the program. If it doesn't work correctly, check all your blocks carefully one at a time until you find the error.

To learn more about building programs with lists and arrays, visit the companion website at www.wiley.com/go/adventuresincoding to watch Chris build a Bird Fact program!

Further Adventures in Coding

Visit Mr. B's code academy to watch a video explaining variables at www.youtube. com/watch?v=_sVtcPgHAjI.

Achievement Unlocked: **Creating memories.**

In the Next Adventure

In the next adventure, you find out how to use operators and work with numbers, text, and logic to create a super fun math quiz!

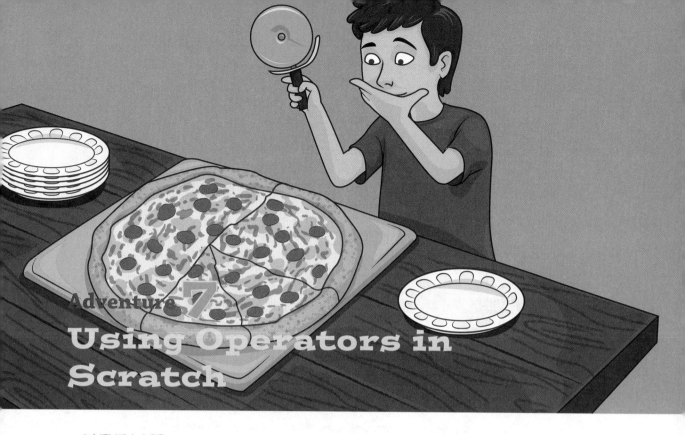

Adventure 7

Using Operators in Scratch

IN THE LAST adventure, you learned about variables and lists in Scratch. Variables and lists are boxes that you use for holding numbers or text. After you have numbers or text in a program, you can do all sorts of things with them, such as adding the numbers together or joining text.

In this adventure, you learn about the Scratch blocks that make it possible to combine, change, add, multiply, divide, and transform variables and values. Welcome to the fascinating world of the operator blocks!

Saying Hello to the Operators

The Operators Block Palette contains 17 blocks. These blocks all have one thing in common: They take one or more values and use them to produce some other value. When you use values to produce other values in programming, it's called "performing an operation." The blocks that make **operations** possible are called "operators."

> **Operations** are specific tasks that work with values to produce results.

Figure 7-1 shows all the operator blocks.

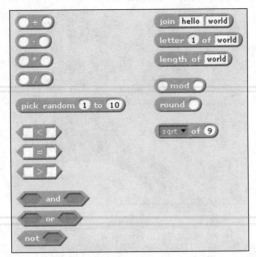

FIGURE 7-1 The operator blocks

Operators are powerful blocks. Understanding and mastering them is the key to being able to do all sorts of useful and essential things in your projects. Some of the things they make possible include

- Keeping score
- Joining words together to customize the things sprites say
- Making sprites move in a realistic way
- Solving math problems
- Checking answers in quiz programs
- Balancing the books in financial projects
- Randomizing the positions and movements of obstacles and monsters in games

You've already used some of Scratch's operator blocks in previous adventures. Read on to learn about each of them and how to use them.

Doing the Math

Math is a huge part of programming. You don't need to be a math genius to write programs, but knowing how to use the math operator blocks certainly makes you look like one! This section shows you how to use each one and gives you some tips, tricks, and examples that you can start using in your own creations today.

Addition

The addition block, shown in Figure 7-2, takes two numbers (or variables containing numbers) and adds them together.

FIGURE 7-2 The addition operator block

To try out the addition block, as well as all the other math operators, you'll be enlisting the help of a puppy. Follow these steps:

1. Click File ➪ New from the top toolbar to create a new project.

2. Click the Choose Sprite from Library icon in the New Sprite menu to open the Sprite Library.

3. Locate the sprite named Dog Puppy and add it to your project.

4. Right-click Scratch the Cat and select Delete to remove her from your project.

5. Drag a when green flag clicked block from the Events Block Palette to the Scripts Area.

6. Drag a forever block from the Control Block Palette and snap it to the when green flag clicked block.

7. Create two new variables in the Data Block Palette. The first one should be called myNumber and the second one should be called myNumber2.

   Your Data Block Palette should now look like Figure 7-3.

8. Right-click myNumber in the Stage.

   Several options for how to display the variable appear, as shown in Figure 7-4.

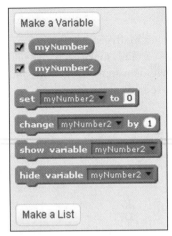

FIGURE 7-3 Creating two variables

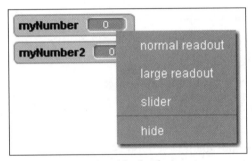

FIGURE 7-4 Variable display options

9. Select slider from the variable display menu.

   The variable display on the Stage turns into a slider, as shown in Figure 7-5.

FIGURE 7-5 A variable slider display

10. Right-click `myNumber2` on the Stage and change it to a slider also.

11. Drag a `think ()` block from the Looks Block Palette to the Scripts Area and snap it inside the `forever` block.

12. Drag a () + () block from the Operators Block Palette and place it into the `think` () block.

13. Drag the `myNumber` variable from the Data Block Palette and place it in the first spot in the () + () block.

14. Drag the `myNumber2` variable from the Data Block Palette and place it in the second spot in the () + () block.

Your script should now look like Figure 7-6.

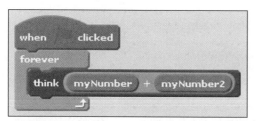

FIGURE 7-6 The finished script

15. Change the title of your project in the space above the Stage to **Addition Puppy** and select File ⇨ Save from the top toolbar.

Click the Green Flag and then click and drag the sliders on your variables on the Stage. The puppy instantly does the math, as you can see in Figure 7-7.

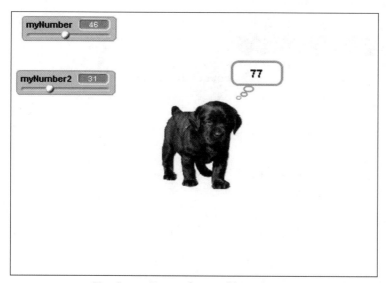

FIGURE 7-7 The Smart Puppy doing addition

Subtraction

Subtraction is just addition in reverse. The () - () block in Scratch is shown in Figure 7-8.

FIGURE 7-8 The subtraction operator block

To create a Subtraction Puppy project, follow these steps:

1. Select File ⇨ Save as a Copy from the top toolbar.

   An exact copy of the project is created, with the title changed to Addition Puppy copy.

2. Change the title of the project to **Subtraction Puppy**.

3. Drag the (myNumber) + (myNumber) block out of the think () block in the Scripts Area, as shown in Figure 7-9.

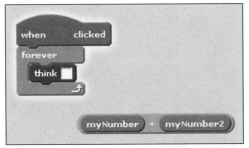

FIGURE 7-9 Dragging the () + () block out of the think () block

4. Drag a () - () block from the Operators Block Palette and drop it into the think () block.

5. Drag the myNumber block from the () + () block in the Scripts Area and place it into the first space in the () - () block.

6. Drag the myNumber2 block from the () + () block in the Scripts Area and place it into the second space in the () - () block.

7. Right-click the empty () + () block and select Delete.

   Your script should now look like Figure 7-10.

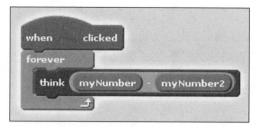

FIGURE 7-10 The Subtraction Puppy script

Test the Subtraction Puppy by clicking the Green Flag and then dragging the variable sliders.

Multiplication

In Scratch, as well as in most other programming languages, the multiplication symbol is the * character. Figure 7-11 shows the Scratch () * () block.

FIGURE 7-11 The multiplication operator block

Here's how to create the Multiplication Puppy program.

1. Select File ⇨ Save as a Copy from the top toolbar.

2. Change the title of the project to **Multiplication Puppy**.

3. Replace the () - () block in the Scripts Area with the () * () block.

   Your finished script should look like Figure 7-12.

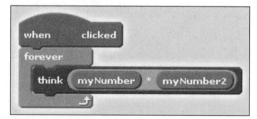

FIGURE 7-12 The finished Multiplication Puppy program

Division

If you're not completely impressed by how fast your puppy can do addition, subtraction, and multiplication, this next display of canine intellect is going to totally win you over.

The Scratch division operator is shown in Figure 7-13.

FIGURE 7-13 The division operator block

To try out the division operator, create the Division Puppy program by following these steps:

1. Create a copy of the Multiplication Puppy program by selecting File ⇨ Save as a Copy from the top toolbar.

2. Change the title of the program to **Division Puppy** and then select File ⇨ Save.

3. Replace the () * () block in the Scripts Area with a () / () block.

   When finished, your script should look like Figure 7-14.

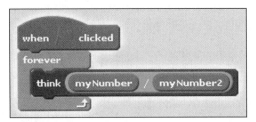

FIGURE 7-14 The Division Puppy program

4. Click the Green Flag and then set both of the number variables to **0** by dragging the slider handles all the way to the left.

   The puppy starts thinking the characters NaN. This stands for Not a Number. In math, we say that the result of dividing 0 by 0 is "no defined value" because there's no way to find an answer for it. Scratch simply says that it's not a number, which is also true.

5. Set the value of the first variable to a number greater than 0, but leave the second number set to 0.

   The puppy starts to think the word Infinity, as shown in Figure 7-15.

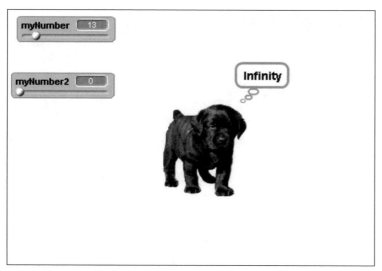

FIGURE 7-15 Division Puppy, contemplating Infinity

When you divide any number by zero, the result is always infinity. For example, if you have a pizza with 12 slices and no one to eat it, how many pieces will each person get and how long will it take to eat? If you have 20 blocks and you want to divide the blocks into groups of 0 blocks, how many groups can you make? There's no way to answer these questions, and no matter how many groups of blocks you have or how long you say it will take to eat the pizza, a larger number is also possible. So, Scratch and the Division Puppy say the value is infinity.

6. Drag the slider for myNumber all the way to the left to set it to **0** and drag the slider for myNumber2 to any number other than 0.

The result is 0. Can you figure out why?

If you have no pizza, it doesn't matter how many people you want to give a slice of pizza to—they'll all get no pizza.

Coding Logically

The Boolean operator blocks each use a value, or multiple values, to decide whether something is true or false. Boolean operating is also known as Boolean logic. You saw the Boolean blocks in Adventure 3, when you learned about their good friends, the condition blocks. To quickly review, the six Boolean blocks in the Operators Block Palette are

- () > (). The *greater than* block produces a value of true if the first number is bigger than the second.

- () < (). The *less than* block produces a value of true if the first number is smaller than the second.

- () = (). The *equal to* block produces a value of true if the values (which may be numbers or text) on both sides of the equals sign are the same.

- () and (). The *AND* block produces a value of true if the statements on both sides of the AND are true.

- () or (). The *OR* block produces a value of true if either statement to the right or to the left of OR is true.

- not (). The *NOT* block produces a value of true if the result of the block inside of it is false.

In Adventure 3, you learned that Boolean blocks are used inside control blocks in order to choose between multiple paths or to decide whether to keep on looping.

In this adventure, you use Boolean operator blocks by themselves to experiment with creating true and false values.

Follow these steps and watch how different operations produce true or false values.

1. Drag a () > () block from the Operators Block Palette to the Scripts Area.

2. Enter **3** into the left side of the () > () block and **2** into the right side.

3. Double-click the (3) > (2) block in the Scripts Area.

    A talk bubble appears next to the block and tells you that the result is true, that 3 is greater than 2, as shown in Figure 7-16.

FIGURE 7-16 Finding out whether the number 3 is larger than the number 2

4. Right-click the () > () in the Scripts Area.

   In addition to the normal right-click options, you also see three more: <, =, and >, as shown in Figure 7-17.

FIGURE 7-17 Additional right-click options

5. Select the less than (<) symbol from the right-click menu.

   Like magic, the () > () block changes into a () < () block, and leaves your values as they were!

6. Double-click the () < () block.

   A talk box appears displaying `false`, showing that 3 is not less than 2.

Using () < (), () = (), and () > () blocks by themselves is pretty simple, but you can also combine them to do much more complicated logic. Follow these steps to see the sorts of things that Scratch can do with logic!

1. Drag a () and () block from the Operators Block Palette to the Scripts Area.

2. Snap your (3) < (2) block into the first space within the () and () block.

3. Drag a () > () block from the Operators Block Palette to the Scripts Area and snap it into the right side of the () and () block.

4. Change the values in the () > () block to **99** and **1**.

5. Double-click the () and () block.

   The result is `false`, as shown in Figure 7-18, because only one of the two halves of the () and () block is true.

6. Drag a () or () block from the Operators Block Palette to the Scripts Area.

7. Drag the (3) < (2) block from the left side of the () and () block to the left side of the () or () block.

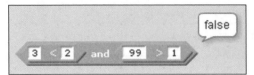

FIGURE 7-18 Only one part is true, so the `()  and  ()` block is false

8. Drag the `(99)  >  (1)` block from the right side of the `()  and  ()` block to the right side of the `()  or  ()` block.

9. Double-click the `()  or  ()` block.

   This block produces a true value because one of the sides of the block is true, as shown in Figure 7-19.

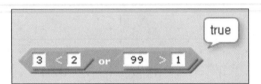

FIGURE 7-19 Only one part is true, so the `()  or  ()` block is true

CHALLENGE

Can you create a `()  or  ()` block in the Scripts Area that will be true if the *x* position of Scratch is greater than 25 or the *y* position of the mouse pointer is less than 0?

Operating on Text

The text operators in Scratch can work with user-entered text, variables containing text, and just plain text in order to figure out how many characters are in it, find letters in text, and join pieces of text together.

Combining Text with join () ()

The `join ()  ()` block lets you combine words, and even sentences, to create custom values to store in variables or to be used by sprites.

A very common use for the `join () ()` block is for mixing the values of variables into things that will be said by a sprite. To use the `join () ()` block to make Scratch the Cat count potatoes, follow these steps.

1. Click File ⇨ New in the top toolbar to create a new project.

2. In the Data Block Palette, create a new variable called **potatoes**.

3. Drag a `when green flag clicked` block from the Events Block Palette to the Scripts Area.

4. Drag the `set () to ()` block from the Data Block Palette and snap it to the `when green flag clicked` block.

5. Make sure that the drop-down menu in the `set () to ()` block is set to potatoes, and that the second space in the block contains a **0**.

6. Drag a `repeat ()` block from the Control Block Palette and snap it to the bottom of the `set (potatoes) to (0)` block.

7. Change the value in the `repeat ()` block to **4**.

8. Drag a `change () by ()` block from the Data Block Palette and snap it inside the `repeat ()` block.

   The drop-down menu should be set to potatoes and the second space should be set to 1.

9. Drag a `say () for () secs` block from the Looks Block Palette and snap it to the bottom of the `change (potatoes) by (1)` block inside the `repeat (4)` block.

10. Drag a `join () ()` block from the Operators Block Palette into the first space in the `say () for () secs` block.

11. Drag the `potatoes` variable from the Data Block Palette and place it inside the first space in the `join () ()` block.

12. Type the word **potato** into the second space in the `join () ()` block.

13. Click the Green Flag to start the counting.

    The result on the Stage should look like Figure 7-20.

You're almost there, but it's strange how Scratch the Cat doesn't have a space between the number and the word *potato*. It's important to remember that Scratch doesn't put in spaces for you when you join words together.

To fix the problem, click your mouse just before the word potato in the second space in the `join () ()` block and press the space bar.

FIGURE 7-20 Joining a variable and text

Now click the Green Flag again, and it looks much better, as shown in Figure 7-21.

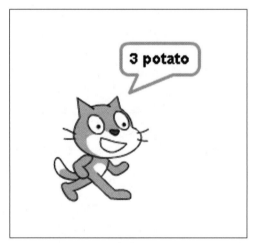

FIGURE 7-21 Don't forget to use spaces!

Finding Letters

The `letter () of ()` block tells you what letter comes at a certain position in a word or text. To use it, follow these steps:

1. Drag a `letter () of ()` block from the Operators Block Palette to the Scripts Area.

2. Enter the number **1** into the first space and your name into the second space in the block.

3. Double-click the block.

   You see a talk bubble with the first letter of your name in it, as shown in Figure 7-22.

FIGURE 7-22 Finding out the first letter in your name!

When you combine the `letter () of ()` block with the `length of ()` block, you can do some pretty cool tricks. Try it out.

Getting Text Length

The `length of ()` block tells you how many characters (including spaces and punctuation) there are in a piece of text.

If you want to find out what the last letter of any person's name is, you can combine the `length of ()` block with the `letter () of ()` block. Try it out:

1. Drag a `letter () of ()` block to the Scripts Area.

2. Drag a `length of ()` block to the Scripts Area and place it inside the first space in the `letter () of ()` block.

3. Type your name into both the `length of ()` block and the `letter () of ()` block, as shown in Figure 7-23.

FIGURE 7-23 A block to get the last letter of a name

4. Double-click this block to find out the very last letter in whatever text you entered into both spaces.

WHAT HAPPENS?

When Scratch runs this combined block, it first determines the result of the `length of ()` block. It then uses this number to determine what letter is in that position. In the preceding example, the result of the `length of ()` block is 5 and the end result is the letter S because S is the fifth letter in the name Chris.

CHALLENGE

Can you figure out how to use a variable and an `ask () and wait` block to make Scratch the Cat ask you your name and then tell you what the last letter of your name is?

Understanding Other Operations

Scratch can go far beyond basic math and logic. The last three blocks in the Operators Block Palette perform math functions that aren't as common as basic arithmetic but are quite common in Scratch programs.

() mod ()

The `() mod ()` block divides the first number by the second number and then tells you what's left over (the remainder). For example, if you make a `(7) mod (3)` block, the result will be 1, because 7 can be divided by 3 twice, with 1 left over.

Figure 7-24 shows the `() mod ()` block in action.

FIGURE 7-24 Using the `() mod ()` block

round ()

The `round ()` block rounds a number to its closest whole number. For example, the block in Figure 7-25 produces a value of 8 because 7.51 is closer to 8 than it is to 7.

FIGURE 7-25 Rounding with Scratch

() of ()

This last mathematical operator block is actually 14 blocks in one! The drop-down menu inside this block has 14 possible values, as shown in Figure 7-26.

FIGURE 7-26 The () of () block has many functions

Explaining how all these functions work and when you might use them is more than we have time for in this book. If you're curious about them, you can read about them on the Scratch website at http://wiki.scratch.mit.edu/wiki/()_of_(). Some of them are involved in advanced mathematics, and they can help you create more natural movements, curves, and lines on the Stage and solve complex problems.

Make a Math Practice Game

In this adventure, you create a math practice game that quizzes you with different math problems and keeps score of how well you did answering ten questions!

The first job in writing this program is to make a sprite ask what type of math you want to practice. You start with addition and multiplication, but you can expand the program later on to include any type of math you want!

1. Select File ⇨ New from the top toolbar to create a new project.

2. Drag a when green flag clicked block from the Events Block Palette to the Scripts Area.

3. Create a new variable in the Data Block Palette called Score.

4. Drag a set () to () block from the Data Block Palette and snap it to the bottom of the when green flag clicked block.

5. Make sure that the first value in the set () to () is **Score** and the second value is **0**.

6. Drag a say () for () secs block from the Looks Block Palette to the Scripts Area and snap it to the when green flag clicked block.

7. Drag another say () for () secs block to the Scripts Area and snap it to the bottom of the previous one.

8. Drag an ask () and wait block from the Sensing Block Palette and snap it to the bottom of the script.

9. Change the value of the first say () for () secs block to **Hello!**

10. Change the value of the second say () for () secs block to **Let's do some math!**

11. Change the question in the ask () and wait block to **Do you want to practice addition or multiplication (enter + or x)?**

12. Your script should now look like Figure 7-27.

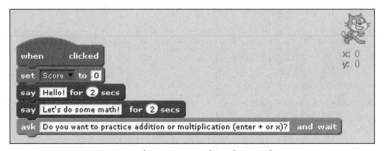

FIGURE 7-27 Getting things started in the math practice program

Programming Different Paths

The next thing you do is to create three different paths the program can take depending on the user's answer to the first question.

- If the user enters +, the program takes the user to the addition quiz.

- If the user enters x, the program takes the user to the multiplication quiz.

- If the user enters anything other than x or +, Scratch the Cat says that she doesn't understand.

To program these three branches, follow these steps:

1. Drag an `if () then, else` block from the Control Block Palette to the Scripts Area and attach it to the `ask () and wait` block.

2. Drag a `() = ()` block from the Operators Block Palette and place it in the hexagram shape in the `if () then, else` block.

3. Drag the `answer` block from the Sensing Block Palette and place it into the left side of the `() = ()` block.

4. Enter the **+** symbol into the right side of the `() = ()` block.

5. Drag an `if () then, else` block into the else part of the first `if () then, else` block, as shown in Figure 7-28.

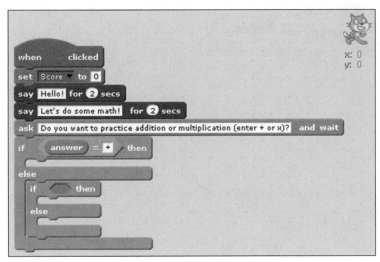

FIGURE 7-28 Creating a nested condition

6. Drag a () = () block into the new `if () then, else` block.

7. Drag an `answer` block into the left side of the () = () block.

8. Enter a lowercase **x** into the right side of the () = () block.

9. Drag a `say () for () secs` block from the Looks Block Palette and drop it into the `else` section of the nested `if () then, else` block.

10. Change the value in the `say () for () secs` block to **I didn't understand your answer.**

11. Your script should now look like Figure 7-29.

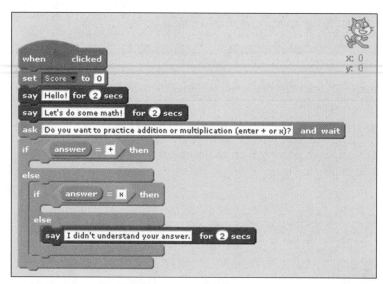

FIGURE 7-29 The conditions are all right

Now you've created the three main branches of the program! Move on to the next section to build the addition quiz.

Making the Addition Quiz

Follow these steps to create a scored Addition Quiz.

1. Drag a `repeat ()` block from the Control Block Palette and drop it into the empty space in the first `if () then, else` block.

2. Create two new variables in the Data Block Palette: **Number1** and **Number2**.

3. Drag a `set () to ()` block from the Data Block Palette and snap it inside the `repeat ()` block.

4. Set the first value in the `set () to ()` block to **Number1**.

5. Drag a `pick random () to ()` block from the Operators Block Palette and snap it into the second space in the `set () to ()` block.

6. Change the second value in the `pick random () to ()` block to **100**.

7. Duplicate the `set () to ()` block you just created and snap it to the bottom of the first one.

8. Change the first value in this new `set () to ()` block to **Number2**.

9. Drag an `ask () and wait` block to the Scripts Area and snap it to the bottom of the `set (Number2) to (pick random (0) to (100))` block.

10. Drag a `join()()` block into the space in the `ask () and wait` block.

11. Drag another `join () ()` block into the second space in the `join () ()` block.

12. Drag one more `join () ()` block into the second space of the last `join () ()` block.

13. Make your `ask () and wait` block look like Figure 7-30.

FIGURE 7-30 The finished addition question

14. Drag an `if () then, else` block to the Scripts Area and snap it to the bottom of the `ask () and wait` block.

15. Drag a `()=()` block into the space in the `if () then, else` block.

16. Drag an `answer` block into the first part of the `() = ()` block.

17. Drag a `() + ()` block into the second part of the `() = ()` block.

18. Snap the `Number1` variable into the first space in the `() + ()` and snap the `Number2` variable into the second space in the `() + ()` block.

19. Drag a `say () for () secs` block inside the space after `then`, in this `if () then, else` block.

20. Change the value of this `say () for () secs` block to **Correct!**

21. Drag a `change () by ()` block from the Data Block Palette and snap it to the bottom of the `say () for () secs` block.

22. Change the first value in the `change () by ()` block to **Score** and change the second value to **1**.

23. Drag a `say () for () secs` block to the Scripts Area and snap it into the `else` part of the `if () then, else` block.

24. Change the value of this `say () for () secs` block to **No, that's not correct.**

CHALLENGE

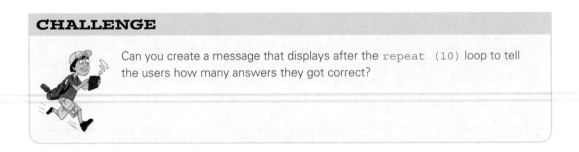

Can you create a message that displays after the `repeat (10)` loop to tell the users how many answers they got correct?

The finished addition quiz, including the answer to the challenge question, is shown in Figure 7-31.

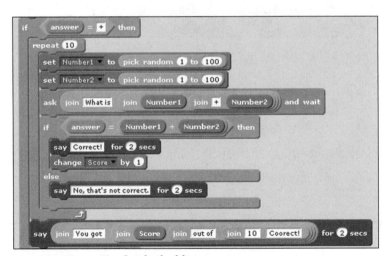

FIGURE 7-31 The finished addition quiz

To learn how to add a feature to the game that will keep track of your score, watch the Adventure 7 video on the companion website at www.wiley.com/go/ adventuresincoding.

Making the Multiplication Quiz

The multiplication quiz is very similar to the addition quiz. The only difference is in the messages that are displayed, and in the values. Set the range for the multiplication quiz from **0** to **12**, so that it's easier for people taking the quiz to do the math in their heads.

Can you create this part of the program yourself? Here are the basic steps:

1. Drag the `repeat ()` block out of the script for a moment, and then duplicate it and place the duplicate into the space after `if (answer = x) then`.

2. Put the original `repeat ()` block back where it was.

3. Modify the contents of the new `repeat ()` block, as well as the `say () for ()` block that follows it and gives the score, to match Figure 7-32.

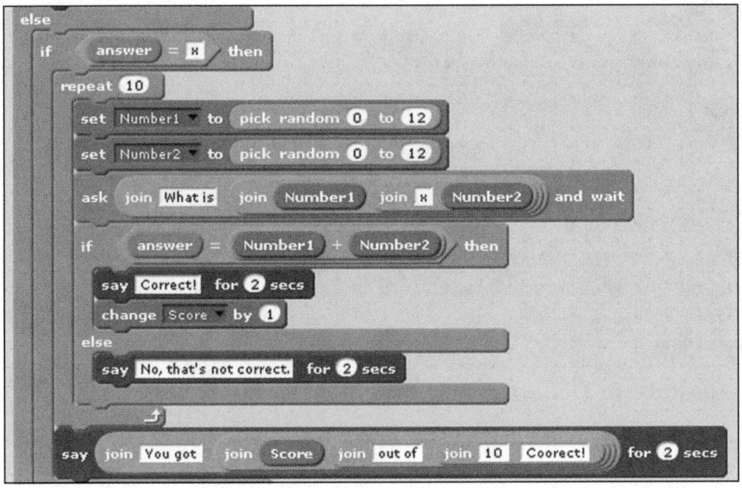

FIGURE 7-32 The finished multiplication quiz

When you're done, the whole program should look like Figure 7-33.

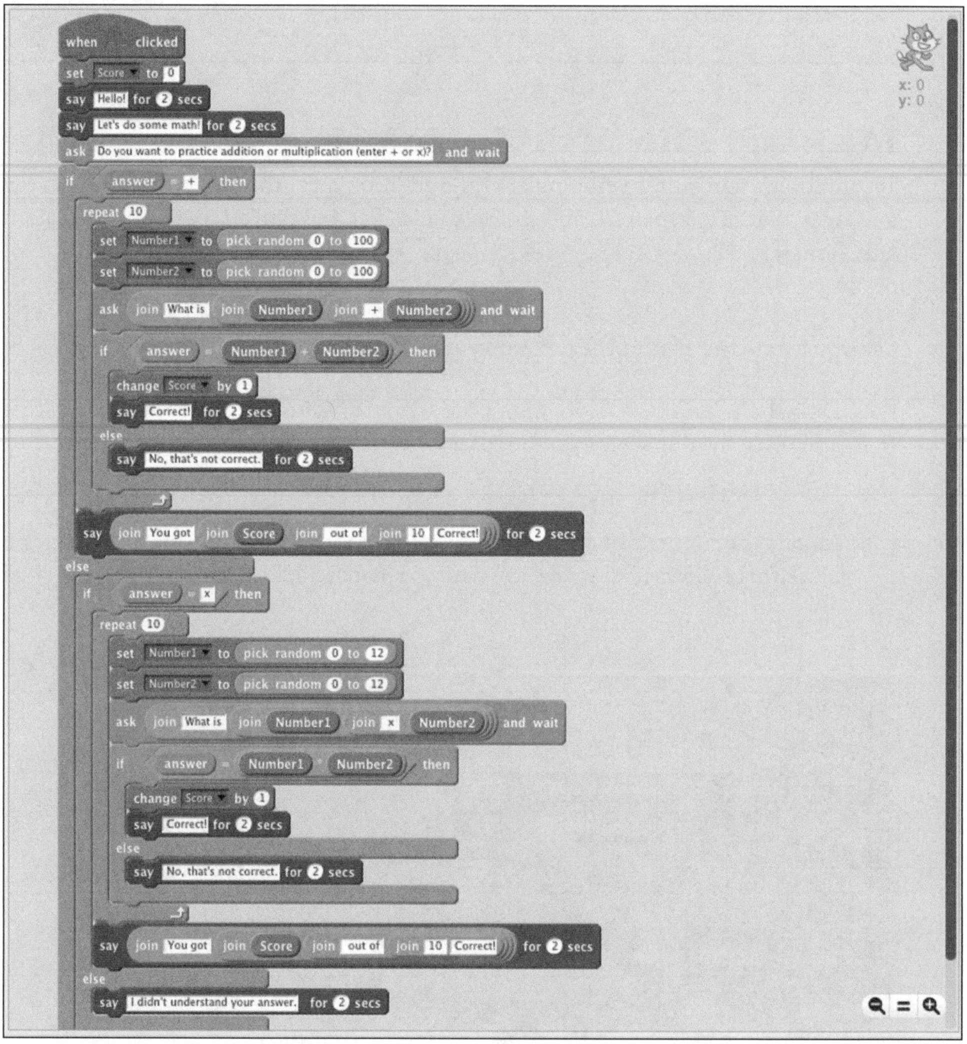

FIGURE 7-33 The finished Math Quiz Program

Further Adventures in Coding

Learn to use operators to create more realistic games by adding gravity and acceleration to a jumping sprite. Visit www.youtube.com/watch?v=4YoGkwV7D9c to watch a video.

Achievement Unlocked: **Performing Operations**

In the Next Adventure

In the next adventure, you find out how you can create amazing art with Scratch. You're introduced to the different ways to use the Paint Editor, and learn how to create interactive art projects!

Using Graphics and the Pen

SCRATCH ISN'T JUST about variables, loops, and operators. It's also a great place to create original interactive art and animations. In this adventure, you discover how to use Scratch to create, change, and animate your own artistic creations.

Creating Art with the Paint Editor

Scratch lets you create your own sprites and backdrops by drawing, painting, and importing graphics from your computer—or even by taking pictures using a camera connected to your computer!

The tool for creating your own graphics is called the Paint Editor. You've worked with the Paint Editor in previous adventures, but in this one, you learn about some more advanced ways to use it. In no time at all, you'll be painting like a pro!

One popular use for the Paint Editor is to create multiple backdrops that can be connected to form a slideshow. Slideshows are a great way to show off several of your artistic creations or to teach new skills. To make a slideshow that teaches people how to make a peanut butter and jelly sandwich, follow these steps:

1. Click File ⇨ New from the top toolbar to create a new project.

2. Give the project a name, such as **How to Make a PB&J Sandwich**, by changing the title above the Stage.

3. Click the Paint New Backdrop icon.

   The Paint Editor opens, with a new backdrop called backdrop2 highlighted, as shown in Figure 8-1. This backdrop is your title slide.

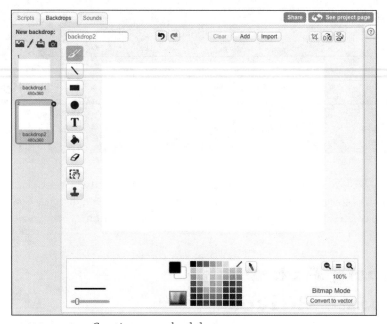

FIGURE 8-1 Creating a new backdrop

4. Select the Text tool, which looks like a capital T, and click in the Paint Area of the Paint Editor, near the upper-left corner.

5. When the cursor appears, type **How to Make a Peanut Butter and Jelly Sandwich**. The text is too long to fit on one line, so press Return or Enter before you type **Peanut Butter and Jelly Sandwich**.

   Your title backdrop should now look similar to Figure 8-2.

6. If your title still has a line around it, that means it's selected. Click somewhere else in the Paint Editor to unselect it.

   When you click outside of the text box, the title appears on the Stage, as shown in Figure 8-3.

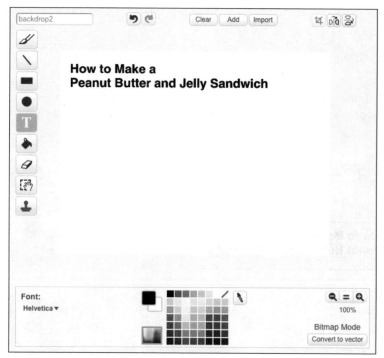

FIGURE 8-2 The start of the title backdrop

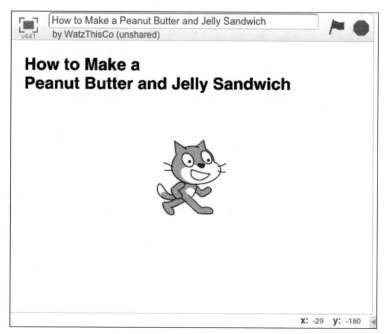

FIGURE 8-3 The title appears on the Stage

7. Click the icon in the Paint Toolbar with the dotted line and the hand. This is the Selection tool.

8. Use the Selection tool to drag a rectangle around all the text in your Paint Editor.

When you finish drawing the rectangle, it turns blue, and squares—called handles—appear at the corners and on the sides, as shown in Figure 8-4.

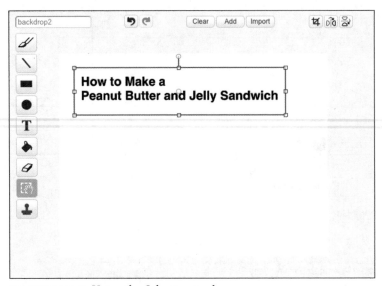

FIGURE 8-4 Using the Selection tool

9. Click and drag the handles on the sides and corners of the selected area to stretch it and make it as big as you want it to be, as shown in Figure 8-5.

Notice how the edges of the text get choppy when you make it bigger? To understand why that happens and how you can fix it, you need to know about the two different ways that you can use the Paint Editor. These are Vector mode and Bitmap mode. Which one you'll use at any one time depends on what kind of art you're creating.

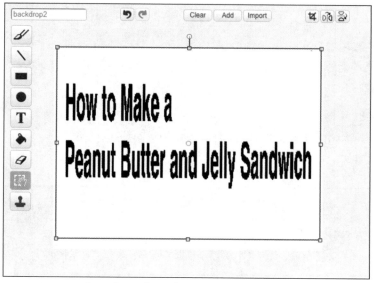

FIGURE 8-5 Stretching the title using the handles

Using Bitmap and Vector Graphics

Whenever you open the Paint Editor to create something new, it opens in Bitmap mode. You know you're in Bitmap mode when your tools are on the left side of the Paint Area.

Understanding the Bitmap Tools

The Bitmap tools let you draw anything you want. They paint shapes, text, lines, and color using tiny squares called **pixels**.

Pixels are tiny dots that make up an on-screen image.

Bitmap tools work really well for editing with photographs or really complicated drawings. They give you precise control over every pixel in an image or graphic.

However, bitmap graphics are made of a certain number of pixels, so when you make them larger, they look distorted, or **pixelated**, as shown in Figure 8-6.

FIGURE 8-6 Bitmap graphics get pixilated when you make them bigger

Pixelated describes the look of an image that has been enlarged to the point where you can see the individual pixels that make up the image.

Another drawback to bitmap graphics is that they don't have the ability to be layered. For this reason, after you create text or a shape using bitmap tools, you can't easily resize or modify them.

When you're working with text or shapes, it's much easier to work with the Paint Editor's other tools, the Vector Drawing tools.

Drawing with the Vector Tools

Vector Drawing tools use lines, rather than pixels, to create graphics. Vector graphics work great for illustrations, text, and shapes.

When you use Vector Drawing tools, you can easily resize shapes and move things around in layers in the Paint Editor. Follow these steps to make a new title slide using the Vector Drawing tools.

1. Click the Paint New Backdrop icon to create a new backdrop.

2. In the lower-right corner of the Paint Editor, click the button that says Convert to Vector.

    Notice that the tools disappear from the left side of the Paint Editor and new tools appear on the right.

3. Find the Vector Text tool, which looks like a capital T, and click it.

4. Click your mouse inside the Paint Area where you want to put some text.

5. Type **How to Make a Peanut Butter and Jelly Sandwich**. You can press Return or Enter to create multiple lines of text that fit in the Paint Area.

If you want, you can change the font and the color by using the Font menu and the Color Palette at the bottom of the Paint Editor. When you're done typing, the title should look similar to Figure 8-7.

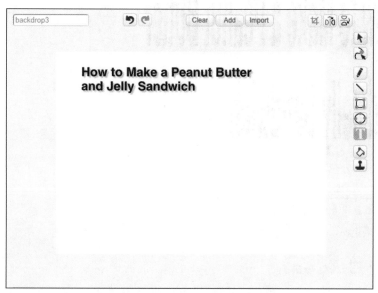

FIGURE 8-7 Creating a title slide with vector text

Notice that vector text has a shadow behind it in the Paint Editor. This is how you can know whether text was written using the Vector Text tool or the Bitmap Text tool.

6. Click the Select tool in the Vector Drawing tools.

It's the tool at the very top, which looks like an arrow.

7. Use the Select tool to click the text in the Paint Area.

Handles appear around the text.

8. Use the handles around the text to resize it to fit the entire Paint Area, as shown in Figure 8-8.

Notice how vector text stays smooth no matter how large you make it or how much you squish and stretch it. This is because it's made up of shapes and lines that can be any size, rather than pixels.

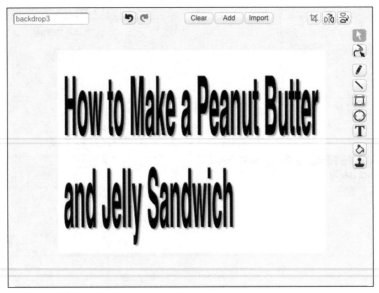

FIGURE 8-8 Resizing vector text

Making Slides

The next step in your slideshow project is to make the slides that tell people how to make this delicious sandwich. Follow these steps.

1. Clean up your backdrops by deleting the blank backdrop and the one with the pixelated title text. Change the name of your title slide to **Title**.

2. Click the Paint New Backdrop icon to make a blank backdrop. Name this backdrop **Bread**.

3. Click Convert to Vector in the Paint Editor to work in Vector mode.

4. Click the Rectangle tool and then select a color that resembles the color of bread from the Color Palette.

5. Draw two squares on your backdrop, as shown in Figure 8-9.

   If you hold down the Shift key as you draw your rectangles, you make perfect squares!

   These will be the pieces of bread for the sandwich.

6. Click the Paint Bucket tool from the toolbar, select a lighter brown color, and click inside each of the bread squares to fill them, as shown in Figure 8-10.

7. Use the Text tool to write **Start with two pieces of bread.** above your bread squares.

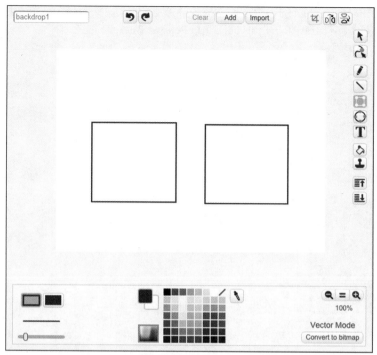

FIGURE 8-9 Drawing bread squares

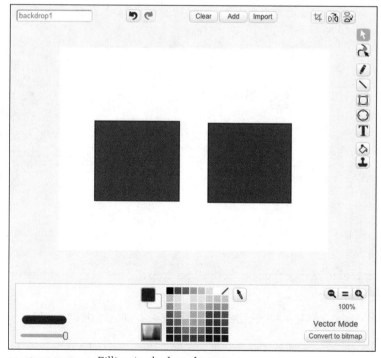

FIGURE 8-10 Filling in the bread squares

8. Right-click the thumbnail of the backdrop you just created and select Duplicate, as shown in Figure 8-11. Name this backdrop **Peanut Butter**.

FIGURE 8-11 Duplicating the bread squares backdrop

9. Select a different brown color to be the peanut butter.

10. Choose the Pencil tool and slide the Pen Size bar to make the widest possible pen, as shown in Figure 8-12.

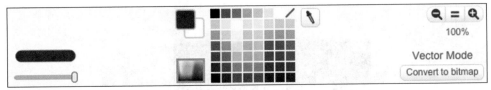

FIGURE 8-12 Making the pen size as big as possible

11. Use the Pencil tool to scribble peanut butter on one slice of bread, as shown in Figure 8-13.

12. Use the Text tool to change the text on this backdrop to **Spread peanut butter on one slice of bread.**

13. Duplicate the peanut butter backdrop. Name this new backdrop **Jelly**.

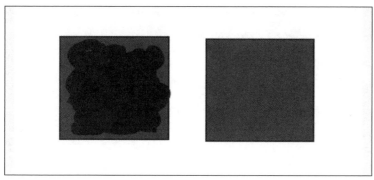

FIGURE 8-13 Scribbling the peanut butter

14. Choose a color for your jelly, and scribble jelly on the other slice of bread, using the Pencil tool.

15. Change the text on this backdrop to **Spread jelly on the other slice of bread.**

    Your project should now look like Figure 8-14.

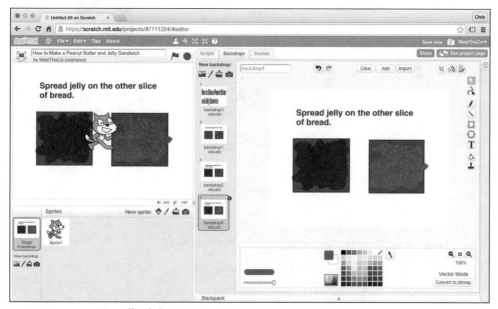

FIGURE 8-14 The jelly slide

16. Duplicate the jelly backdrop. Name it **Combine**.

17. Change the text on the new backdrop to **Put the bread with peanut butter on the bread with jelly.**

18. Next duplicate the bread backdrop. Name this one **Done**.

19. Use the Select tool to select one of the pieces of bread.

20. Delete the selected slice of bread.

21. Move the sandwich to the center of the Paint Editor.

22. Change the text on this backdrop to **Enjoy your sandwich!**

    This completes your backdrops for the project. Your project should look like Figure 8-15.

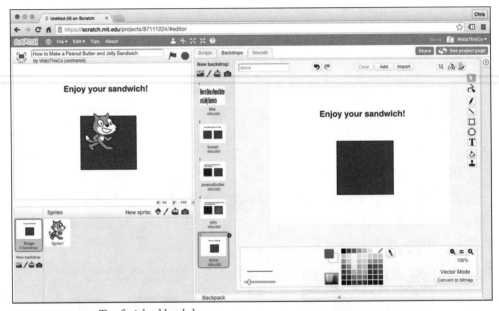

FIGURE 8-15 The finished backdrops

Next, you write a script to make the slides change. Follow these steps.

1. Click the Scratch the Cat sprite in the Sprites Pane.

    The Costume Editor appears, with Scratch the Cat in the middle of it.

2. Click the Scripts tab at the top of the Costume Editor.

3. Drag a when green flag clicked block from the Events Block Palette to the Scripts Area.

4. Drag a switch backdrop to () block from the Looks Block Palette and snap it to the when green flag clicked block.

5. Change the drop-down menu in the switch backdrop to () block to **Title**.

6. Drag a `when () key pressed` block from the Events Block Palette to the Scripts Area.

7. Change the drop-down menu in the `when () key pressed` block to Space.

8. Drag a `switch backdrop to ()` block from the Looks Block Palette and snap it to the bottom of the `when () key pressed` block.

9. Change the drop-down menu in the `switch backdrop to ()` block to **Next Backdrop**.

Your script should now look like Figure 8-16.

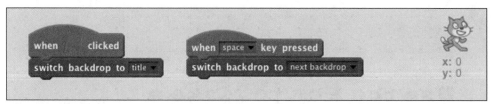

FIGURE 8-16 The finished slideshow script

10. Right-click Scratch the Cat in the Sprite Pane and select Hide, as shown in Figure 8-17.

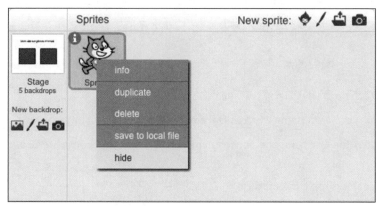

FIGURE 8-17 Hiding Scratch the Cat

Click the Green Flag to start your slideshow and press the space bar to go through each of the slides!

Can you figure out how to add music to the slideshow so that it starts playing when you press the Green Flag?

VIDEO

To watch Eva complete the PB&J sandwich slideshow, visit the companion website at `www.wiley.com/go/adventuresincoding` and choose Adventure 8!

Use the Pen to Make a Skywriting Plane

Scratch's Pen blocks make it possible for you to write programs that create graphics and help you to draw pictures on the Stage.

You saw an example of code that draws using the pen in the random drawing program in Adventure 2. In this adventure, you use the pen to create a skywriting plane program that draws in the sky with clouds as you move your mouse around the Stage.

Figure 8-18 shows what the finished program will look like on the Stage.

To code the Skywriting app, follow these steps:

1. Select File ⇨ New from the top toolbar.

2. Give your new project a name, such as **Daredevil Skywriting**.

3. Delete Scratch the Cat from the Sprites Pane so that you can choose a custom sprite.

4. Click Choose Backdrop from Library.

   The Backdrop Library opens.

5. Find the Blue Sky sprite and click it. Click OK to add it to your project.

6. Click the Choose Sprite from Library icon in the Sprites Pane.

   The Sprite Library opens.

7. Locate the Airplane sprite and add it to your project.

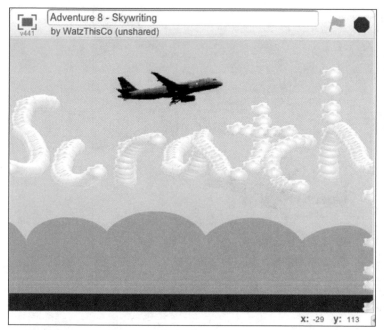

FIGURE 8-18 Drawing with clouds

8. Click the Choose Sprite from Library icon in the Sprites Pane again and add the Cloud sprite to your project.

   Your program should now look like Figure 8-19.

Now that the Stage is set, your first task is to make this plane fly wherever your mouse goes on the Stage.

1. Click the Airplane sprite in the Sprites Pane to open its Scripts Area.

2. Drag a `when green flag clicked` block from the Events Block Palette to the Scripts Area.

3. Drag a `forever` block from the Control Block Palette to the Scripts Area and snap it to the `when green flag clicked` block.

4. Drag a `go to ()` block from the Motion Block Palette and snap it inside the `forever` block.

5. Change the value in the drop-down menu in the `go to ()` block to **Mouse-pointer.**

FIGURE 8-19 The Stage and sprites are set

Your script should now look like Figure 8-20. Click the Green Flag and move your mouse around the Stage to see how the airplane follows it.

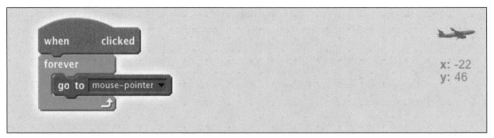

FIGURE 8-20 The script to make the airplane follow the mouse

Next, you add a script to the cloud to make it follow the plane and draw wherever the plane goes!

1. Click the Cloud sprite in the Sprites Pane to view its Scripts Area.

2. Use the Shrink tool from the top toolbar to shrink the cloud until it's small enough to fit inside the plane, as shown in Figure 8-21.

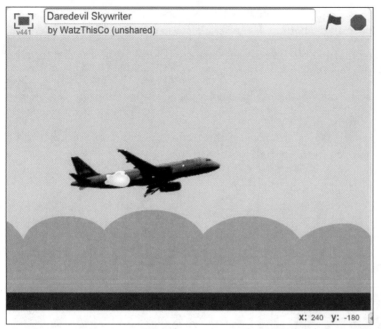

FIGURE 8-21 Making the cloud fit in the plane

3. Drag a `when green flag` clicked block from the Events Block Palette to the Scripts Area.

4. Drag a `go back ()  layers` block from the Looks Block Palette and snap it to the `when green flag clicked` block.

   This block causes the cloud to hide behind the airplane.

5. Drag a `clear` block from the Pen Block Palette and snap it to the bottom of the `go back ()  layers` block.

   The `clear` block erases the previous drawing every time you press the Green Flag.

6. Drag a `forever` block from the Control Block Palette to the Scripts Area and snap it to the `go back ()  layers` block.

7. Drag a `go to ()` block from the Motion Block Palette and snap it inside the `forever` block.

8. Change the drop-down menu in the `go to ()` block to **airplane**.

   This causes the cloud to follow the plane around.

9. Drag an `if () then` block from the Control Block Palette and snap it inside the `forever` block, to the bottom of the `go to (airplane)` block.

10. Drag a `mouse down?` block from the Sensing Block Palette and snap it into the hexagonal space in the `if () then` block.

11. Drag a `stamp` block from the Pen Block Palette and snap it inside the `if (mouse down?) then` block.

The `stamp` block causes an image of the sprite (the cloud, in this case) to be drawn, or stamped, at the current location of the sprite.

The finished cloud script looks like Figure 8-22.

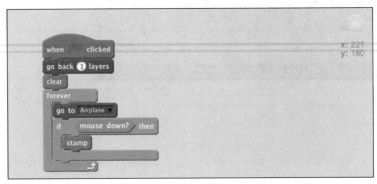

FIGURE 8-22 The finished cloud script

Now press the Green Flag to try it out!

CHALLENGE

 Can you write your name with the skywriting plane? What other kinds of pictures can you draw?

Further Adventures in Coding

Achievement Unlocked: **Scratch Artist**

Bloom, by ykoubo, is a great starter project that you can copy and modify to create interesting flower patterns. You can check it out by going to `https://scratch. mit.edu/projects/2546637/`. Take a look at the other projects (in the Remixes pane) that are based on this program and then try making your own!

To find out more about bitmap and vector images, go to Scratch class at `https:// scratch.mit.edu/projects/10568936/`.

In the Next Adventure

In the next adventure, you find out how to make your very own blocks! Making your own blocks is the key to creating complex programs in Scratch with less work. You also learn how to share scripts between different programs using the Backpack.

Adventure 9
Building Your Own Blocks

SO FAR, YOU'VE been using Scratch's built-in blocks and they're great, but Scratch also lets you make your own blocks that you can personalize and customize to your particular needs. In this adventure, you use custom blocks and a handy tool called the Backpack to put on a fashion show!

Making Your Own Blocks

If you can dream it up, you can probably create it by using Scratch's built-in blocks. But, sometimes, your programs can get pretty complicated, with many different blocks all put together in a very precise way.

When that happens, a great way to stay organized and make programming easier is to create your own **custom blocks**.

Custom blocks are single blocks that represent a group of blocks, or script. You can use a custom block in your program to stand for a larger piece of code.

Let's take another look at the arrow key sprite control script that you created in Adventure 4, which is shown in Figure 9-1.

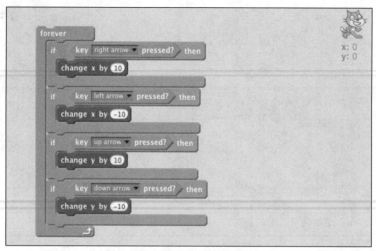

FIGURE 9-1 Basic arrow key controls

That's a lot of blocks to just make a sprite move around when you press the arrow keys. Wouldn't it be great if there were a block like the one shown in Figure 9-2 that you could use to do the same thing as all of the blocks in Figure 9-1?

FIGURE 9-2 An arrow key movement block

Well, there can be, and you can make it yourself! We show you how to create custom blocks in the next section.

Splitting Programs into Custom Blocks

You've learned about and used a lot of different blocks so far, in each of the different categories in the Block Palette. There's one very special category of the Block Palette where you can create an unlimited number of custom blocks. This is called the More Blocks Palette. To make your first custom block, follow these steps.

1. Select File ⇨ New from the top toolbar to start a new project.

2. Click the More Blocks category in the Block Palette.

   You see two buttons in the More Blocks Block Palette, as shown in Figure 9-3.

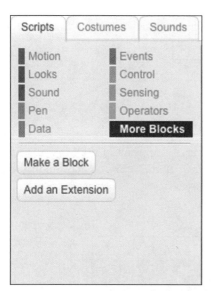

FIGURE 9-3 The More Blocks Block Palette

3. Click Make a Block in the More Blocks Block Palette.

   The New Block pop-up window opens, as shown in Figure 9-4.

FIGURE 9-4 The New Block pop-up window

4. Enter **Draw Circle** into the text area in the New Block pop-up window, as shown in Figure 9-5.

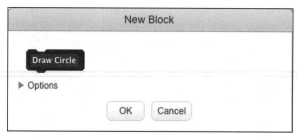

FIGURE 9-5 Naming a new block

5. Click OK to create your new block.

A new stack block with the name `Draw Circle` appears in the More Blocks Block Palette, and a hat block named `define Draw Circle` appears in the Scripts Area. Both of these are shown in Figure 9-6.

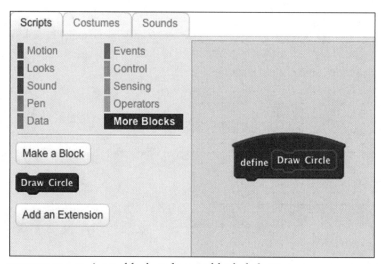

FIGURE 9-6 A new block and a new block definition

Next you need to define what the `Draw Circle` block will do. Everything under the custom block's hat block will run every time you use the custom stack block.

Follow these steps to define the `Draw Circle` block and make it actually draw a circle.

1. Drag a `pen down` block from the Pen Block Palette to the Scripts Area and snap it to the `define Draw Circle` block.

2. Drag a `repeat ()` block from the Control Block Palette and snap it to the bottom of the `pen down` block.

3. Change the value in the `repeat ()` block to **180**.

4. Drag a `move ()` `steps` block from the Motion Block Palette and snap it inside the `repeat ()` block.

5. Change the value in the `move ()` `steps` block to **1**.

6. Drag a `turn clockwise ()` `degrees` block from the Motion Block Palette and snap it to the bottom of the `move ()` `steps` block.

7. Change the value in the `turn clockwise ()` `degrees` block to **2**.

   Your `define Draw Circle` block script should now look like Figure 9-7.

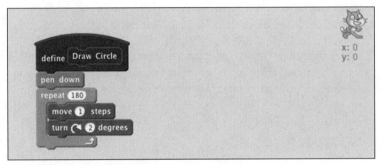

FIGURE 9-7 Defining the `Draw Circle` custom block

8. Drag a `Draw Circle` custom block from the More Blocks Block Palette to the Scripts Area.

9. Double-click the `Draw Circle` block in the Scripts Area.

   Scratch the Cat moves and draws in a circle.

10. Use your mouse to drag Scratch the Cat to a different location on the Stage.

11. Double-click the `Draw Circle` block in the Scripts Area.

   Scratch the Cat draws another circle, starting in the new location.

Are you curious about how the `Draw Circle` block works? The key is that there are 360 degrees of directions in a circle. In this code, your sprite first moves forward one step and then changes direction by 2 degrees. Since there are 360 degrees in a circle, the sprite needs to turn 2 degrees 180 times (because 180 times 2 is 360).

CHALLENGE

Can you figure out how to make a larger circle? If you don't know now, read on to find out in the next section!

Changing Custom Blocks

Your new `Draw Circle` block is pretty awesome. Anywhere where your sprite is on the Stage, when the `Draw Circle` block runs, it causes the sprite to draw a circle.

But it can only draw one size of circle, in one color. Wouldn't it be great if you could draw different circles with this same block? You can! All you need to do is modify your custom block so that you can tell it what kind of circle to draw. Here's how:

1. Click the More Blocks Block Palette.

   You see your custom block, `Draw Circle`.

2. Right-click the `Draw Circle` block and select Edit, as shown in Figure 9-8.

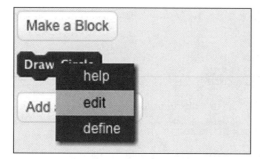

FIGURE 9-8 Editing a custom block

The Edit Block pop-up window opens, as shown in Figure 9-9.

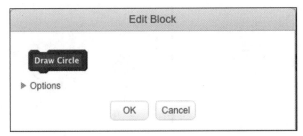

FIGURE 9-9 The Edit Block pop-up window

3. Click the arrow next to Options in the Edit Block pop-up window.

    You see the custom block options, as shown in Figure 9-10.

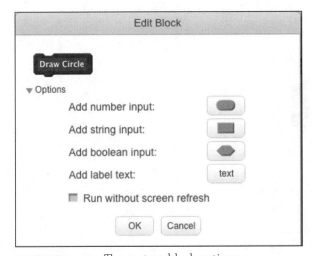

FIGURE 9-10 The custom block options

4. Click the oval icon to the right of the words Add Number Input.

    An oval appears in the image of your custom block inside the pop-up window, as shown in Figure 9-11.

5. Change the name of the number input to **size** by typing inside the oval.

6. Click OK to save your block.

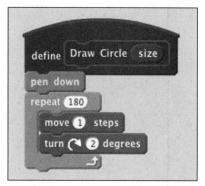

FIGURE 9-11 Adding a number input to the `Draw Circle` block

Take a look at your block definition in the Scripts Area now. You see that it has a new block called `size` next to the name of the block, as shown in Figure 9-12.

FIGURE 9-12 Adding a number input to the `Draw Circle` block

You also notice that your custom stack block now has a place in it for entering a number, as shown in Figure 9-13.

Draw Circle ①

FIGURE 9-13 The `Draw Circle` block with a number input

Try changing the number in the Draw Circle () block in your Scripts Area to a larger number, such as **4**, and then double-click it.

Did you see what happened? No? That's right! Nothing changed.

In order for the number in the Draw Circle () block to do anything, you need to use your new variable size inside of your script.

1. Click the size oval inside the define Draw Circle () hat block.

2. Drag the size oval to the move () steps block and snap it inside of the oval between move and steps.

Your custom block definition should now look like Figure 9-14.

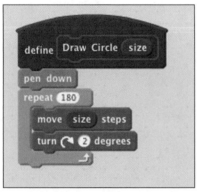

FIGURE 9-14 Using a number input inside a custom block

When you send a value into a custom block from the outside, that's called "passing an argument". It's not the kind of argument that you might have with your friend, though. In programming, an *argument* is any value that is sent into (or "passed into") a program, such as size is in this example.

3. Change the value of the number input in the Draw Circle () stack block to **3** and double-click it.

Scratch the Cat draws a larger circle on the Stage, as shown in Figure 9-15.

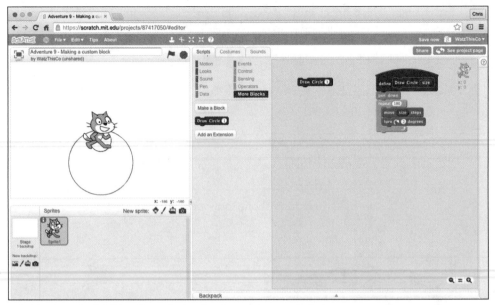

FIGURE 9-15 Making Scratch the Cat draw a larger circle

After you have a custom block, you can use that same custom block with any sprite by dragging the custom block definition onto the new sprite. Follow these steps to try it out:

1. Click Choose Sprite from Library in the Sprite Pane.

   The Sprite Library opens.

2. Select any sprite that you like and click OK to add it to your project.

3. Click Scratch the Cat in your Sprite Pane to view Scratch the Cat's Scripts Area.

4. Click the `define Draw Circle ()` hat block in the Scripts Area and drag it onto the image of your new sprite in the Sprite Pane.

5. Click your new sprite in the Sprite Pane.

   You see a copy of the `define Draw Circle ()` block in the Scripts Area, and the `Draw Circle` block in the More Blocks Block Palette, as shown in Figure 9-16.

6. Drag a `Draw Circle ()` block from the More Blocks Block Palette to the Scripts Area.

7. Double-click `Draw Circle()`.

   Your new sprite draws a circle of the size that you specify in the number input.

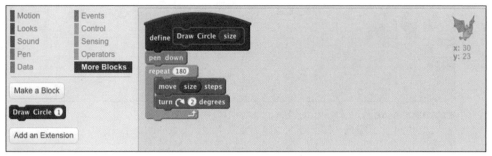

FIGURE 9-16 Copying a custom block to a new sprite

Now you know how to share custom blocks between sprites in the same program. But, what if you want to share a custom block (or any script, for that matter) between two different projects?

That's where Scratch's Backpack comes in.

Borrowing Blocks with the Backpack

The Backpack in Scratch is an area where you can store custom blocks and scripts that you create in one program so you can use them in other programs. To access the Scratch Backpack, you need to be signed into your account. If you haven't already created an account, please refer to Adventure 1 for more information.

While you're working within Scratch, the Backpack is always waiting there at the bottom of the screen, as shown in Figure 9-17.

FIGURE 9-17 The Backpack is at the very bottom of the Scratch Project Editor

When you click the up arrow on the Backpack bar, the Backpack Pane expands to show a new blank area of the Scratch Project Editor, as shown in Figure 9-18.

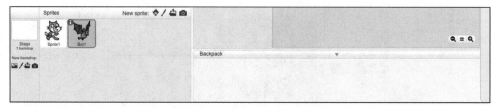

FIGURE 9-18 The expanded Backpack Pane

Here's how to use the Backpack to carry your `Draw Circle ()` custom block, or any other custom block, with you into a new program.

1. Open the Scripts Area, if it's not open already, by clicking the Scripts tab at the top of the Project Editor.

2. Click and drag your `define Draw Circle ()` block definition from the Scripts Area into the Backpack.

   A copy of the `define Draw Circle ()` block definition appears in the Backpack, as shown in Figure 9-19.

FIGURE 9-19 Copying a custom block definition to your Backpack

3. Select File ⇨ New from the top menu bar to create a new program.

4. Click the up arrow to expand the Backpack Pane.

   You see the `define Draw Circle ()` custom block definition inside your Backpack.

5. Drag the `define Draw Circle ()` custom block definition from the Backpack and drop it into the Scripts Area in your new program.

6. Open the More Blocks Block Palette.

   You see your custom `Draw Circle ()` block.

7. Drag a `Draw Circle ()` block to the Scripts Area.

8. Double-click the `Draw Circle ()` block in the Scripts Area to make your sprite draw a circle.

The Backpack and custom blocks are great tools for helping you to get more done with less coding—which is one of the most important skills for a programmer to learn!

Learn more about borrowing custom blocks using your Backpack by visiting the companion website at www.wiley.com/go/adventuresincoding and choosing Adventure 9!

Putting on a Fashion Show

Now it's time to put together everything you've learned about custom blocks to organize a Scratch Fashion Show. In this program, sprites use a custom block to walk or dance toward the camera, showing off their different costumes on the way.

1. Select File ➪ New from the top toolbar to start a new project.

2. Name your project **Fashion Show** by typing into the text area above the Stage.

3. Click Choose Backdrop from Library in the Stage Sprite Pane.

4. When the Backdrop Library opens, find the backdrop named Clothing Store, select it, and add it to your project.

5. Click Scratch the Cat and go to her Scripts Area by clicking the Scripts tab, if necessary.

6. Open the More Blocks Block Palette.

7. Click the Make a Block button.

    The New Block pop-up window appears.

8. Name the new block **Fashion Walk** and click OK to close the New Block pop-up window and create the new block.

9. Drag a `set size to () %` block from the Looks Block Palette to the Scripts Area.

10. Set the value in the `set size to ()%` to **20**.

11. Drag the `Fashion Walk` block from the More Blocks Block Palette to the Scripts Area.

12. Double-click the `Fashion Walk` block in the Scripts Area.

    Scratch the Cat shrinks down to 20% of her normal size.

13. Drag Scratch the Cat on the Stage to a place where it looks like she's standing at the very back of the room, as shown in Figure 9-20.

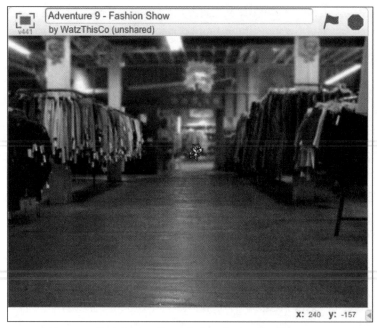

FIGURE 9-20 Positioning Scratch the Cat on the Stage

14. Drag a `go to x: () y: ()` block from the Motion Block Palette to the Scripts Area and snap it to the `set size to ()%` block.

    Because you just positioned Scratch the Cat, the block already contains the correct values for *x* and *y*.

15. Drag a `show` block from the Looks Block Palette to the Scripts Area and snap it to the bottom of the `go to x: () y: ()` block.

16. Drag a `repeat ()` block from the Control Block Palette and snap it to the bottom of the `show` block.

17. Change the value of the `repeat ()` block to **20**.

18. Drag a `wait () secs` block from the Control Block Palette and snap it inside the `repeat ()` block.

19. Change the value in the `wait () secs` block to **0.1**.

20. Drag a `change size by ()` block from the Looks Block Palette and snap it to the bottom of the `wait () secs` block.

21. Set the value of the `change size by ()` block to **5**.

22. Drag a `change y by ()` block from the Motion Block Palette and snap it to the bottom of the `change size by ()` block.

23. Change the value of the change y by () block to **–5**.

24. Drag a next costume block from the Looks Block Palette and snap it to the bottom of the change y by () block.

25. Drag a glide () secs to x: () y: () block to the Scripts Area and snap it to the bottom of the repeat () block.

26. Enter the values **2, 273,** and **–71** in the glide () secs to x: () y: () block.

27. Drag a hide block from the Looks Block Palette to the Scripts Area and snap it to the bottom of the glide () secs to x: () y: () block.

28. Drag a wait () secs block to the Scripts Area and snap it to the bottom of the hide script.

Your Scripts Area should now look like Figure 9-21.

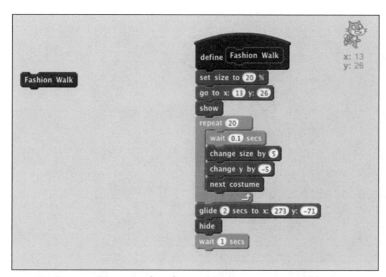

FIGURE 9-21 The completed Fashion Walk custom block

29. Double-click the Fashion Walk custom block on the Stage and watch as Scratch the Cat walks toward the camera and then glides off to the right!

Now you're almost done! The next steps are to add several more sprites to the Stage and give them all the same Fashion Show custom block.

1. Click Choose Sprite from Library in the toolbar above the Sprite Pane.

2. When the Sprite Library opens, locate the sprite named Dan and add it to your project.

3. Repeat Steps 1 and 2 to add the sprite named Breakdancer1 to your project.

4. Click the Scratch the Cat sprite in the Sprite Pane to view Scratch the Cat's Scripts Area.

5. Click the `define Fashion Walk` custom block definition hat block. Drag it to the Sprite Pane and drop it on the Dan sprite.

6. Drag the `define Fashion Walk` custom block definition to the Breakdancer1 sprite in the Sprite Pane.

7. Click each of the sprites to make sure that they all have the `Fashion Walk` custom block.

8. Click Scratch the Cat in the Sprite Pane.

9. Drag a `when green flag` clicked block from the Events Block Palette and snap it to the top of the `Fashion Walk` custom block, as shown in Figure 9-22.

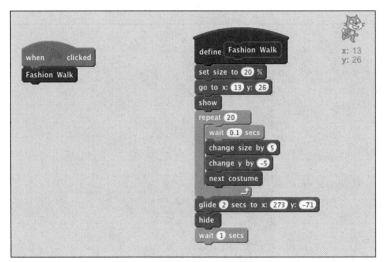

FIGURE 9-22 Starting the fashion show when the Green Flag is clicked

10. Drag a `broadcast ()` block from the Events Block Palette and snap it to the bottom of the `Fashion Walk` stack block.

   You use broadcast events to tell the other sprites to start their fashion walks.

11. Click the drop-down in the `broadcast ()` block and choose New Message.

12. Set the new message to **Dan**.

13. Click the Dan sprite in the Sprite Pane to open its Scripts Area.

14. Drag a `when green flag clicked` block from the Events Block Palette to the Scripts Area.

15. Drag a `hide` block from the Looks Block Palette to the Scripts Area and snap it to the `when green flag clicked` block.

16. Drag a `when I receive ()` block from the Events Block Palette and drop it in the Scripts Area.

17. Change the value in the `when I receive ()` block to **Dan**.

18. Drag the `Fashion Walk` block from the More Blocks Block Palette and snap it to the `when I receive ()` block.

19. Drag a `broadcast ()` block from the Events Block Palette and snap it to the bottom of the `Fashion Walk` block.

20. Select New Message. from the `broadcast ()` block and add a new message of **Breakdancer1**.

In the next steps, you make the break dancer walk!

1. Click Dan in the Sprite Pane to open the Scripts Area.

2. Drag the script starting with the `when green flag clicked` block and drop it onto the thumbnail of the Breakdancer1 sprite in the Sprite Pane.

3. Drag the script starting with `when I receive ()` and drop it onto the thumbnail of the Breakdancer1 sprite in the Sprite Pane.

4. Click the thumbnail image of the Breakdancer1 sprite in the Sprite Pane.

   If the sprite's scripts are overlapping, drag them to rearrange them in the Scripts Area.

5. Disconnect the `broadcast () block` from the bottom of the `Fashion Walk` custom block and drag it out of the Scripts Area.

   Because this is the last sprite to do its fashion walk, it doesn't need to broadcast to any other sprites.

6. Change the value of the `when I receive ()` block to **Breakdancer1**.

7. Click the Green Arrow and enjoy the show!

Further Adventures in Coding

Check out custom blocks created by other people that you can use in your own programs at the Block Library at `http://blocklibrary.weebly.com/`.

Achievement Unlocked: **Custom Blocks**

In the Next Adventure

In the next adventure, you learn how to make and use music in Scratch! You can play music, record sounds, compose songs, and much more—and then use these sounds as background music or as actions in response to events!

Adventure 10
Making and Using Sounds and Music

IN THIS ADVENTURE, you explore the sounds of Scratch. More importantly, you learn how to use Scratch to record, play, and compose music! So, turn up your speakers (or put on your headphones) and let's get started!

Using Sounds

The place where all of Scratch's music and sound blocks live is in the Sound Block Palette, shown in Figure 10-1.

You can use the blocks in the Sound Block Palette to play sounds from the Sound Library, to play recorded sounds (even those that you record yourself), and to compose melodies by picking instruments and stringing notes together.

FIGURE 10-1 The Sound Block Palette

The Sound Library

Are you looking for that perfect sound for a sprite to make when it's doing a particularly complex dance move? How about the sound of laughing or even of sneezing to add more realism to your project?

The Scratch Sound Library contains more than 100 sounds that you can use in your programs. These include a rooster crow, cat meows, cheering, and all sorts of musical instruments.

Before you can use any of these awesome sounds, you need to add them to your project in the same way that you add sprites and backdrops. It's time to go to the library and check out some sounds. Go to the Scratch Project Editor and follow these steps:

1. Select File ⇨ New from the top toolbar to create a new project.

2. Click the Sounds tab to open the Sound Editor, as shown in Figure 10-2.

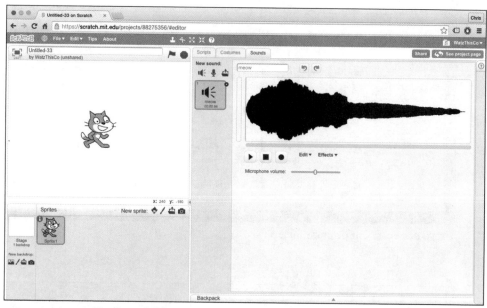

FIGURE 10-2 The Sound Editor

3. Click the Choose Sound from Library icon in the New Sound menu, which looks like a speaker.

   The Sound Library opens, as shown in Figure 10-3.

4. Browse through the library and click the arrows to the right of the sounds you want to hear.

5. Find a sound you like and click it to select it. Click OK to add the sound to the sound palette for the current sprite, as shown in Figure 10-4.

Follow these steps to make your sprite play this new sound.

1. Click the Scripts tab to open the Script Editor and the Block Palette.

2. Drag a `when this sprite clicked` block from the Events Block Palette to the Scripts Area.

3. Drag a `play sound ()` block from the Sound Block Palette to the Scripts Area and snap it to the bottom of the `when this sprite clicked` block.

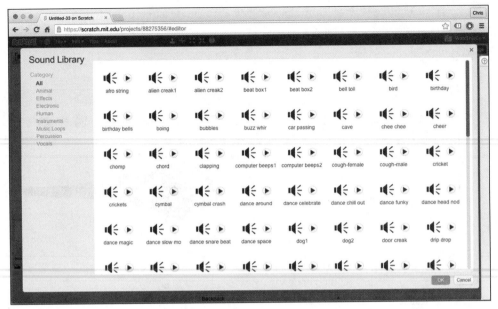

FIGURE 10-3 The Sound Library

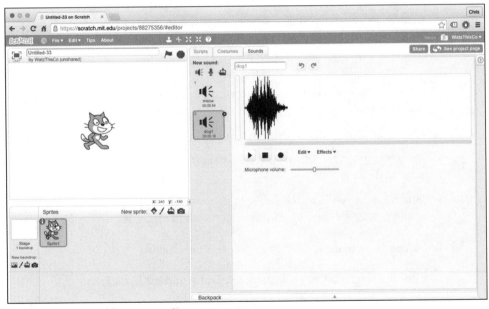

FIGURE 10-4 Adding a sound to your sprite

4. Change the drop-down menu in the `play sound ()` block to the sound that you added from the Sound Library.

5. Click Scratch the Cat on the Stage to play the new sound!

The Sound Library has a lot of sounds, but you're not limited to just these sounds. You can edit and change the sounds in the library and you can also upload and use any sound you can record or find on the web. You find out how to add custom sounds to your project in the next sections.

Using the Sound Editor

The Sound Editor is where you can view your sounds as waveforms, record new sounds, edit sounds, and apply effects to sounds.

A **waveform** is the visual representation of a sound.

To find out more about the Sound Editor, click the Sounds tab. You see the name of the selected sound, followed by a waveform diagram of that sound.

You can tell a lot about a sound from its waveform. The length of the waveform tells you how long the sound will play. The height of the waveform tells you how loud or quiet the sound is. The shape of the waveform tells you how complex the sound is.

Compare the waveform for the sound called Pop, shown in Figure 10-5, with the waveform for the sound called Computer Beeps3, shown in Figure 10-6.

FIGURE 10-5 The Pop sound

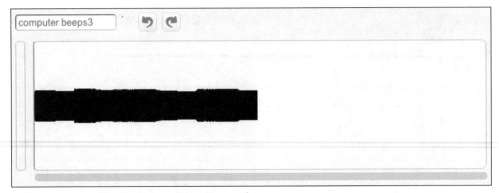

FIGURE 10-6 The Computer Beeps3 sound

CHALLENGE

What can you tell about these two sounds just by looking at their waveforms? Without listening to them, can you tell three differences between how they'll sound when you play them?

Editing Sounds

Using the tools below the waveform, you can edit any sound to make it louder, quieter, shorter, and even longer!

Follow these steps to customize one of Scratch's sounds!

1. Select the Meow sound in the Sound Palette.

   You see the sound's waveform.

2. Click and drag your mouse over the waveform to select it, as shown in Figure 10-7.

3. Click the Play button underneath the waveform to hear how Meow sounds.

4. While the waveform is selected, click the Effects drop-down menu and select Reverse.

   Notice that the waveform flips over, as shown in Figure 10-8.

5. Press the Play button now to hear a backward cat sound!

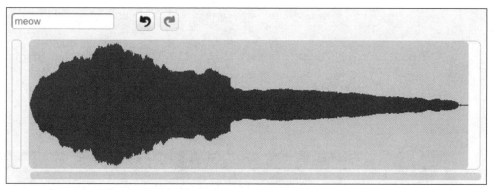

FIGURE 10-7 Selecting a sound's waveform

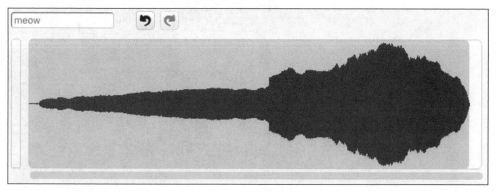

FIGURE 10-8 Reversing a sound

You can also select and edit any part of a sound. For example, you can use the Sound Editor to make part of a sound louder or quieter, to make sounds fade in or out, and even to copy and paste parts of sounds into other sounds.

Recording Sounds

If you have a microphone connected to your computer, you can use the Sound Editor to record your own voice or sounds!

To record a sound from your computer's microphone, follow these steps:

1. Click the Record New Sound icon (it looks like a microphone) in the Sound Palette.

   A new blank sound opens in the Sound Editor.

2. Click the round icon under the waveform box in the Sound Editor. This is the Record button.

   You see a pop-up window, as shown in Figure 10-9, asking whether Scratch can have access to your computer's microphone.

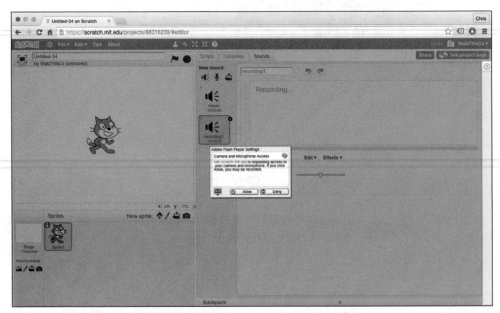

FIGURE 10-9 Scratch asks for permission to use your microphone

3. Click the Allow button.

4. The first time you use the microphone with Scratch, you see another pop-up window asking you again if it's okay for Scratch to use your microphone. Choose OK here, too.

   Scratch starts recording.

5. When you're done recording, press the square icon (the Stop icon) to the left of the Record button to stop recording.

   If your sound was recorded successfully, you see a waveform in the Sound Editor, as shown in Figure 10-10, and you can click the Play icon to play back your sound.

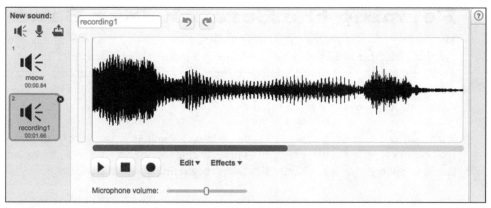

FIGURE 10-10 A recorded sound in the Sound Editor

Importing Sounds

The last button under New Sound in the Sound Palette is the Upload Sound from File button. Using this button, you can find any sound file or music file on your computer and turn it into a sound inside Scratch that you can play inside your projects.

To import a sound, click the Import Sound from File button in the Sound Editor and then find any sound or music file on your computer and click Open. The new sound appears in your Sound Editor and is available to use with the sprite you imported it into.

If you want to import music that was created by someone else and play it in your projects, make sure that it's okay with whoever created the file first! Copying other people's music without asking for permission and giving proper credit isn't polite. As long as your project is just for educational purposes, you're not prohibited from using other people's songs (this is a concept called "fair use"), but it's always nice to ask first whenever possible.

To watch a video about using the Scratch Sound Editor, visit the companion website at www.wiley.com/go/adventuresincoding and choose Adventure 10!

Forming the Scratch Jazz Band

Most of the blocks inside the Sound Block Palette are for making your own music. You can think of these blocks as being very similar to an electronic keyboard. There are 21 different instruments and 18 different drums for you to choose from, and you can vary the speed of the music (its tempo), insert pauses (called rests), and change how loud or quiet the music plays (its volume).

With a little creativity and work, it's possible to assemble Scratch blocks to make sprites work together to make beautiful music. In this section, you use Scratch's sound blocks to put together a jazz band and play the beginning of an old standard.

The song you'll be assembling is one of the most famous songs in all of jazz: "Autumn Leaves."

"Autumn Leaves" was originally a French song called "Les Feuilles Mortes" written in 1945 by Joseph Kosma. In 1947, Johnny Mercer wrote English lyrics to the song. Since then, it's been recorded hundreds of times by different artists.

Tuning Up Your Instruments

The first step in getting the band together is to put the sprites on the Stage. Follow these steps:

1. Select File ⇨ New from the top toolbar to create a new project.

2. Click Choose Sprite from Library from the New Sprite menu.

3. Locate the sprite named Guitar Bass from the Music and Dance category and add it to your project.

4. Click Choose Sprite from Library again and add the Microphone sprite to your project.

5. Click Choose Sprite from Library one more time and add the Drum1 sprite to your project.

6. Remove Scratch the Cat from your project by using the Delete tool or right-clicking Scratch the Cat.

   You should now have three sprites on your Stage. Arrange them in any way you want, as shown in Figure 10-11.

Now that you have a band, let's give them something to do. We'll start with the drummer.

FIGURE 10-11 The sprites for the Scratch Jazz Band project

Finding a Drummer

Jazz drumming uses a special type of beat called a "swing beat." A swing beat is difficult to simulate with a computer program, but you can do a reasonably good job with the Scratch music blocks. Follow these steps to program a simulated swing beat.

1. Click the Drum1 sprite in the Sprite Pane to open the Scripts Area for the drum.

2. Drag a `play drum () for () beats` block from the Sound Block Palette to the Scripts Area.

3. Change the value of the first drop-down menu to **(2) Bass Drum**.

4. Change the value of the second drop-down menu to **0.66**.

5. Drag a `rest for () beats` block from the Sound Block Palette to the Scripts Area and snap it to the bottom of the `play drum (2) for (0.66) beats` block.

6. Change the value in the `rest for () beats` block to **0.66**.

7. Drag a `play drum () for () beats` block from the Sound Block Palette to the Scripts Area and snap it to the `rest for (0.66) beats` block.

8. Change the value of the first drop-down menu in the `play drum () for () beats` block to **2** and the value of the second drop-down menu to **0.66**.

9. Drag another `play drum () for () beats` block to the Scripts Area and change its values to **(6) Closed High Hat** and **0.66 beats**.

10. Drag another `rest for () beats` block to the Scripts Area, snap it to your script, and change its value to **0.66 beats**.

11. Snap another `play drum () for () beats` block to the bottom of the script and change its values to **(6) Closed High Hat** and **0.66 beats**.

12. Drag a `repeat () block` from the Control Block Palette and surround the entire drum script with it.

13. Change the value in the `repeat ()` block to **8**.

Your drum script should now look like Figure 10-12.

FIGURE 10-12 The drum script

Playing the Melody

Here's how to make the script that will play the melody.

1. Click the Guitar sprite in the Sprite Pane to open the Guitar Scripts Area.

2. Drag a `when green flag clicked` block from the Events Block Palette to the Scripts Area.

3. Drag a `set tempo to () bpm` block from the Sound Block Palette, snap it to the `when green flag clicked` block, and set its value to **145**.

In music, the tempo is how fast or slow a song is. BPM stands for "beats per minute." A clock ticks off seconds at 60 bpm. So, a bpm of 145 is a little faster than twice the speed of the second hand on a clock.

4. Drag a `set instrument to ()` block from the Sound Block Palette and snap it to the `set tempo to (145)` bpm block.

5. Select the **(4) Guitar** from the instrument drop-down menu.

The next part of the song you're programming has 17 notes. Most of these play for one beat. Follow these steps to program all 17 notes.

1. Drag a `play note () for () beats` block to the Scripts Area.

2. Change the value of the second number in the `play note () for () beats` block to **1**.

3. Make 11 copies of this block so that you have a total of 12 `play note () for () beats` blocks.

4. Make four groups of three linked blocks, as shown in Figure 10-13.

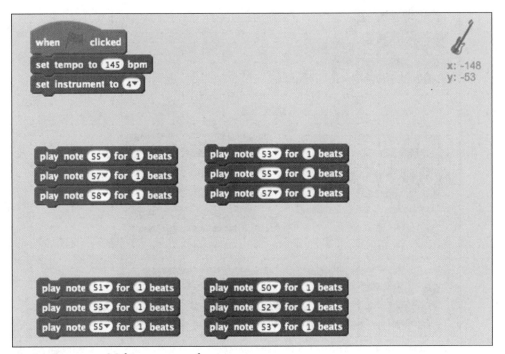

FIGURE 10-13 Making groups of notes

5. Set the notes for all the `play note () for () beats` blocks to the values shown in Figure 10-13.

6. Double-click each group of blocks, one at a time. You should notice that the notes in each group get higher, but each group of three notes starts on a lower note.

7. Drag a new `play note () for () beats` block from the Sound Block Palette and snap it to the bottom of the first group of three.

8. Set the note in this block to **Eb (63)** and the number of beats to **5**.

9. Drag a new `play note () for () beats` block from the Sound Block Palette and snap it to the bottom of the second group of three (the one that starts on note 53).

10. Set the note in this block to **D (62)** and the number of beats to **2**.

11. Drag another new `play note () for () beats` block from the Sound Block Palette and snap it to the bottom of this same group of notes.

12. Set the note in this block to **D (62)** and the number of beats to **3**.

Your guitar sprite's Scripts Area should now look like Figure 10-14.

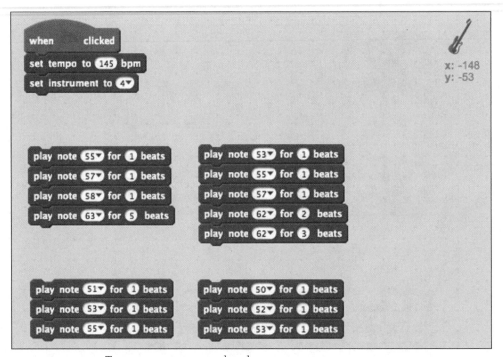

FIGURE 10-14 Two note groups completed

13. Drag a `play note () for () beats` block from the Sound Block Palette to the bottom of the third group (starting with 51) and set its note to **Middle C (60)** and its beats value to **5**.

14. Drag a `play note () for () beats` block from the Sound Block Palette to the bottom of the fourth group (starting with 50) and set its note to **Bb (58)** and its beats to **5**.

Now you have all the notes programmed to play the first four lines of "Autumn Leaves." If you double-click them in order, you can hear how the song goes.

In the next section, you program the timing between the players in the band.

Playing Together

Broadcasting blocks and event blocks can be used to coordinate between different scripts and sprites. In this section, you make the drummer start drumming and the singer start singing.

The first step is to start the drums at the right time. In this song, you want the drummer to start after the first three notes are played by the guitar. Follow these steps to program the guitar to broadcast messages to the other instruments.

1. Separate the last note in the first group of notes from the other three.

2. Drag a `broadcast ()` block from the Events Block Palette and snap it to the bottom of the third note in the first group.

3. Select New Message from the `broadcast ()` block and create a new message with the word **drum**.

4. Click the Drum1 sprite in the Sprites Pane to view the drum sprite's script.

5. Drag a `when I receive ()` hat block from the Events Block Palette and snap it to the top of the Drum1 sprite's script.

6. Select the drum message from the `when I receive ()` hat block's drop-down menu.

7. Click the Guitar Bass Sprite in the Sprites Pane to return to the Guitar Bass sprite's script.

8. Snap the note that you removed from the bottom of the first group to the bottom of the `broadcast (drum)` block.

9. Double-click on the first group of notes.

    The drums should start playing when after the third note plays.

Next, you program the events that cause the singer to sing each line of the song. The first four lines of "Autumn Leaves" are

The falling leaves

Drift by the window

The autumn leaves

Of red and gold

Each of these lines should be sung along with each of the groups of notes. Follow these steps to program the singing!

1. Drag a `broadcast ()` block to the top of each group of three notes.

   You'll be using these broadcast blocks to tell the singer when to sing each line of the song.

2. Create a new message for each of these new broadcast blocks. The four messages should be **falling leaves**, **window**, **autumn leaves**, and **red and gold**.

   When you're finished, your guitar Scripts Area should look like Figure 10-15.

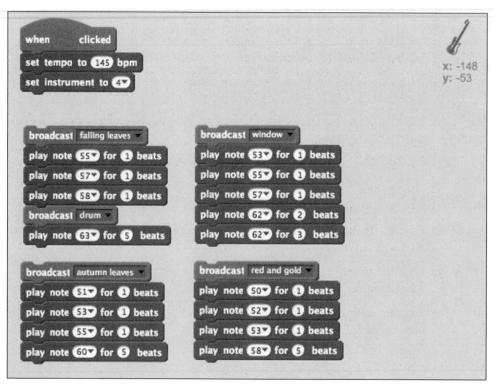

FIGURE 10-15 The guitar script with broadcasts

3. Snap the five pieces together into one script.

   The falling leaves broadcast block should snap to the `set instrument to (4)` block. The window broadcast block should snap to the bottom of that. Then comes the piece that starts with the autumn leaves, and finally the section that begins with the red and gold broadcast block.

When the blocks are linked together, they should look like Figure 10-16.

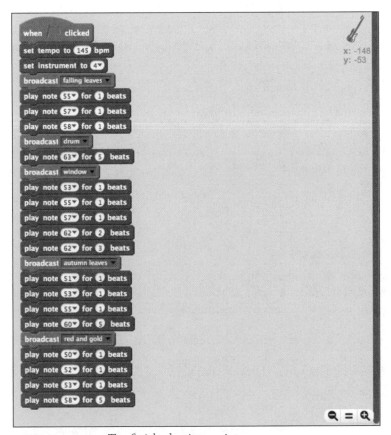

FIGURE 10-16 The finished guitar script

In the next steps, you use the broadcasted messages from the guitar to trigger the microphone sprite to say the lines of the song. Follow these steps:

1. Click the Microphone sprite in the Sprite Pane.

2. Drag four `when I receive ()` blocks from the Events Block Palette.

3. Select falling leaves in the first `when I receive ()` block.

4. Drag a `say ()` block from the Looks Block Palette, snap it to the first `when I receive (falling leaves)` block, and change its value to **The falling leaves**.

5. Select window in the second `when I receive ()` block.

6. Drag a `say ()` block from the Looks Block Palette, snap it to the `when I receive (window)` block, and change its value to **Drift by the window**.

7. Select autumn leaves in the third `when I receive ()` block.

8. Drag a `say ()` block from the Looks Block Palette, snap it to the `when I receive (autumn leaves)` block, and change its value to **The autumn leaves**.

9. Select red and gold in the fourth `when I receive ()` block.

10. Drag a `say () for () secs` block from the Looks Block Palette and snap it to the `when I receive (red and gold)` block.

11. Change the first value in this `say () for ()` block to **Of red and gold** and change the second value to **4**.

12. Click the Green Flag to see and hear your finished jazz band program do its thing!

Singing Along!

After you have the melody and drums in place, you can play the song and sing along. Or, if you have a microphone connected to your computer, you can record yourself singing along and hear it every time you press the Green Flag!

Follow these steps to record your lyrics and add them to the band:

1. Click the Microphone sprite in the Sprite Pane.

2. Click the Sounds tab to open the Sound Editor.

3. Click the Record New Sound icon.

4. Click the Record button and start singing!

5. When you're done singing, click the Stop button.

6. Name your sound.

If everything worked correctly, you see a waveform for your singing in the Sound Editor, as shown in Figure 10-17.

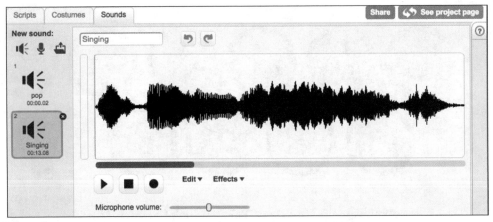

FIGURE 10-17 The new singing sound

7. Play back the sound. If it has any silence at the beginning, select it and use Edit ⇨ Cut to delete it.

You want the singing to start as soon as the Green Flag is clicked.

8. Click the Scripts tab to open the Scripts Area for the Microphone sprite.

9. Drag a `when green flag clicked` block from the Events Block Palette to the Scripts Area.

10. Drag a `play sound ()` block from the Sound Block Palette and snap it to the `when green flag clicked` block.

11. Select your singing sound in the drop-down menu for the `play sound ()` block.

12. Click the Green Flag to hear yourself singing along with the music!

How did you do? Does it sound amazing? If not, try again! Unfortunately, Scratch doesn't give us a way to play the song while we're singing, so you just need to experiment. But, that's what Scratch is all about! Play around with it and have fun!

Further Adventures in Coding

Want to find cool new sounds to use in your projects? Check out Free Sounds at https://freesound.org/, where you can find hundreds of different sounds that are all free to download and use. You can even record and upload your own sounds to freesound.org!

Achievement Unlocked: **The Sounds of Scratch Music**

> ## In the Next Adventure
> In the next adventure, you explore the Scratch universe and learn about remixing, using Scratch with real-life objects, and more!

Exploring the Scratch Universe

SCRATCH IS MORE than a programming language and tool for learning to program. It's also a community of kids and teachers who share their work online and help each other to become better programmers.

This adventure shows you some of the riches that are available for learning about Scratch and coding with Scratch. We show you how to "remix," and we give you tips on how to ask for help when you get stuck with a particularly difficult problem.

Visiting scratch.mit.edu

The `scratch.mit.edu` website, where you've been spending so much time throughout this book, is just the tip of the iceberg when it comes to resources for learning to program. It is the center of the Scratch world, though, and so we're starting there.

When you visit `scratch.mit.edu`, you see the Create button in the top menu. You know by now that this link takes you to the Scratch Project Editor. Right next to it is the Explore link, as shown in Figure 11-1. Click this link now.

FIGURE 11-1 The Explore link

The Explore section at `scratch.mit.edu` shows a categorized gallery of projects created and shared by other Scratch programmers. Anyone who has a confirmed Scratch account can share projects. After you share a project, it may show up in the Explore gallery.

Before you share your first project, take a minute to complete your Scratch Profile, if you haven't done so already. Here's how:

1. Log into `scratch.mit.edu` and click your username in the upper-right corner of the Scratch website. Select Profile.

2. You see your Scratch Profile, similar to Figure 11-2.

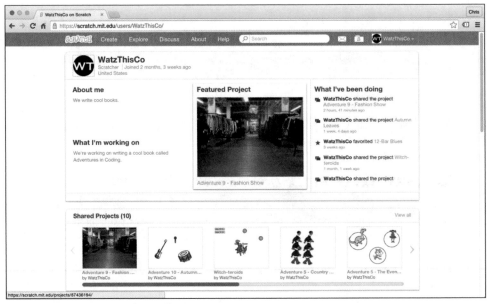

FIGURE 11-2 A Scratch Profile

If you're a brand new Scratch user, your profile says that you're a New Scratcher. After you've been active on the Scratch website for a couple weeks, you get an invitation to upgrade to being a full Scratcher. Upgrading is free.

3. Review the information on your profile and update it now if you want to.

Sharing Your Projects

Now that you have a completed profile, you're ready to show the world your unique creations! To share your Scratch projects, follow these steps.

1. If you're not already logged in, go to `scratch.mit.edu` and log in to your account.

2. Select My Stuff from the drop-down menu underneath your username in the upper-right corner of the screen.

   The My Stuff screen appears, as shown in Figure 11-3. This screen lists all the projects that you've created.

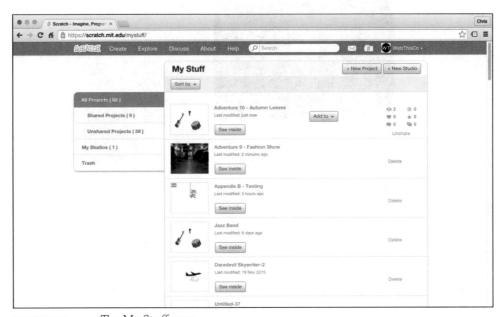

FIGURE 11-3 The My Stuff page

The My Stuff page lists everything, even the mistakes and abandoned projects that you never meant to keep around. It's quite common to have a lot of projects in here that are not totally done, or maybe that you haven't even really started! Fortunately, the inventors of Scratch provided an easy-to-find Delete button to the right of every project to help you keep things tidy.

3. Scroll through your list of projects and find one that you're particularly proud of.

4. Click the title of the project you want to share.

The project page for that program opens, as shown in Figure 11-4. You see a message at the top of the project page that tells you that the project isn't shared.

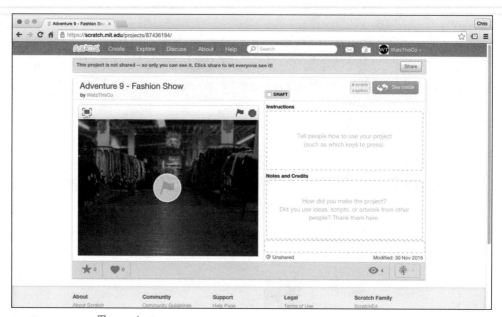

FIGURE 11-4 The project page

5. Click the Green Flag at the top of the Stage or the Green Flag in the middle of the Stage to run your program and to make sure that it's ready for you to share.

If everything looks good, the next step is to fill out the **metadata** for the project. Metadata is information that describes a program. When you create a Scratch program, you can provide metadata that includes

- Instructions
- Notes and credits
- Project tags

Metadata is information used to describe a program. It can contain information such as the creator of the project, the tags associated with your project, or instructions on how to use your program. Metadata is not part of your code, but rather describes the details of your project.

Filling out the project metadata is a very important step in the process of sharing Scratch programs, and you should always be sure to add something to these boxes. Adding metadata is your chance to tell other Scratch users about your program and to make sure that it shows up in the right category in the Explore pages.

Follow these steps to fill out your project's metadata:

1. Click your mouse inside the box under Instructions. Enter some brief directions about how to use the program.

   For example, for the Fashion Show project from Adventure 9, we might provide the following Instructions:

   ```
   Click the Green Flag and watch the show!
   ```

2. Click your mouse inside the Notes and Credits box and enter information about who created the program or anything else that you want someone viewing the project to know about it.

   For example, for the Fashion Show project, our Notes and Credits look like this:

   ```
   From Adventure 9 of Adventures in Coding by Chris Minnick
      and Eva Holland. This project demonstrates how to use
      custom blocks.
   ```

3. Click your mouse inside the Add Project Tags box underneath the Notes and Credits box.

   Several choices appear underneath the box.

4. Choose the most appropriate tags from the list.

   For example, for the Fashion Show, we selected Animations.

If your project fits in more than one of these categories, feel free to choose more than one, but don't choose tags that aren't appropriate to your project.

Our project, with the metadata filled in, is shown in Figure 11-5.

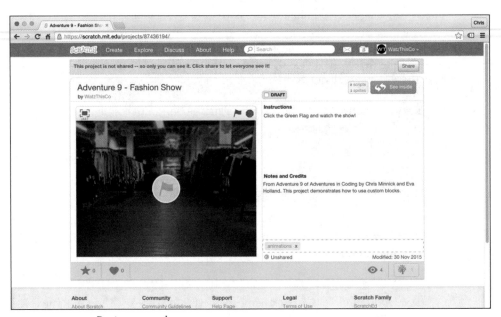

FIGURE 11-5 Project metadata

When you're happy with how your project page looks, click Share at the top of the page. After a moment, the page reloads and you see a new message at the top of the page saying that your project is now shared, as shown in Figure 11-6.

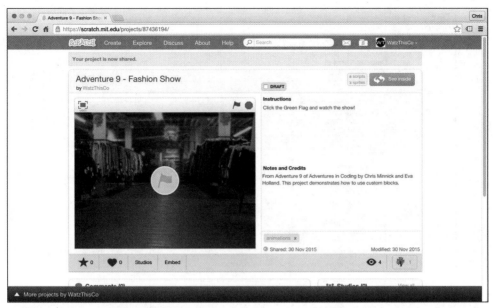

FIGURE 11-6 A shared project

The Scratch Community Rules

The Discuss link at the top of the Scratch website is how you access the Scratch forum. Here, you can get help with your projects, read announcements from the Scratch Team, show off your work, work with other Scratchers, and more!

Anyone with a confirmed Scratch account can participate in discussions in the forums. If you're new to the forums, we recommend that you start out in the New Scratchers forum, shown in Figure 11-7. If your profile says New Scratcher, you're not able to post images or links in the Scratch Forums, and you aren't able to edit your posts.

Take a look at the posts at the top of the New Scratchers forum. They tell you things like "How to Become a Good Scratcher" and the very important "Basic Forum Guidelines."

Just like with any group or place you visit, the Scratch Forum has rules and guidelines that you should follow to make sure that everyone has a good time. Some of the guidelines include

- Keep your posts relevant. If a discussion is about custom blocks, for example, don't ask questions about the Paint Editor in that discussion. There's probably a better place that's just right for that question.

- Keep topics relevant. Make sure that any new topics you create in the forums are related to the category where you post them.

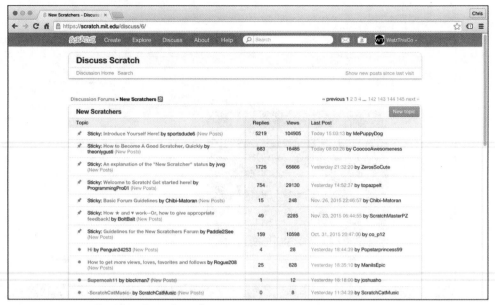

FIGURE 11-7 The New Scratchers forum

- Read Sticky posts. If a forum has topics that are marked as "Sticky," those posts will always appear first in the forum. These are posts that the Scratch Team considers to be very important, and you should always take the time to read them.

After you've read the Sticky posts in the New Scratchers forum, follow these steps to make your first post to the forum!

1. Go to the New Scratchers Forum by clicking the Discuss link at the top of the Scratch website and then clicking New Scratchers.

2. Click the first post in the New Scratchers forum, which is called "Introduce Yourself Here."

3. Read some of the other posts from New Scratchers to get an idea of what sort of things to say.

4. Scroll to the bottom of the page and look for the New Reply area, which looks like Figure 11-8.

5. Write a message! Say "Hi!" and tell your fellow Scratchers why you're learning to code, what your username means (if it has any special meaning to you), and maybe even a little bit about what kinds of projects you hope to make and how you're learning.

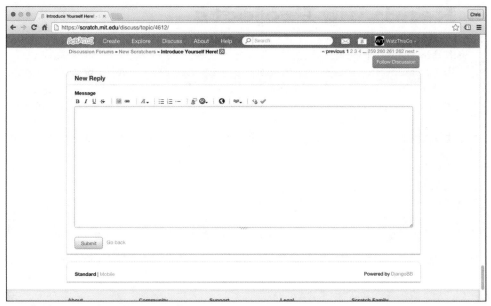

FIGURE 11-8 The New Reply area

If you're enjoying our book so far, we'd appreciate if you'd mention that you're reading *Adventures in Coding!*

6. Try out some of the buttons above the text area in the New Reply area to see what they do.

7. When you're happy with your post, click Submit.

Great job! You're on your way to being a valuable and respected member of the Scratch community. Keep up the great work, keep learning, and have fun!

It's likely that people will write comments on your profile page or "follow" you to welcome you to Scratch. Remember that as you become a more experienced Scratch user, it's always nice to stop in to the New Scratchers forum and welcome some new members now and then!

Remixing Projects

By sharing your project on Scratch, you're agreeing that it can be viewed, copied, and modified by anyone else in the Scratch community. Everyone else agrees to the same thing. This is part of what makes Scratch so much fun! You can look at other people's projects, see how they work, and then improve on them or change them as you want. It's polite, and common practice, to thank the original author in your Notes and Credits, of course.

This process of making a copy and adding your own unique code to a project is what's known in Scratch as **remixing**.

DEFINITIONS

Remixing is the process of producing a different version of something. In the case of Scratch, it means to make a copy of someone's project and make changes to it!

Follow these steps to try remixing a project:

1. Visit the Scratch Studio we created for this book.

   You can find us by going to the Explore section of the Scratch site and searching for WatzThisCo, or by going directly to `https://scratch.mit.edu/studios/1505618/`. You see our Studio, which looks similar to Figure 11-9.

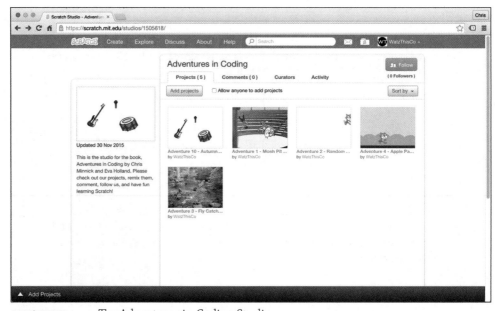

FIGURE 11-9 The Adventures in Coding Studio

2. Click any one of our projects to view its project page.

3. Click the See Inside button in the upper right of the project page to view the blocks and sprites that make up our project.

4. Click the Remix button above the Scripts Area.

A copy of the project is created and added to your My Stuff area.

After you create a copy, visit its project page. Notice that the original project is given credit just under the Notes and Credits area, and a note appears asking you to add a note thanking the original creator of the project and explaining what you added or changed, as shown in Figure 11-10.

FIGURE 11-10 Giving credit where credit is due

Remixing is an important and exciting part of the Scratch universe. Done correctly, it benefits both the original creator (who gets new ideas and improvements from remixers) and the person doing the remixing (who gets to learn from examining and working with other people's code)!

Interfacing with the Real World

Another great feature of Scratch is its ability to work with devices connected to your computer. Remember how we told you way back in Adventure 1 that computer programs are also known as "software"? In this section, we're going to talk about **hardware**. Hardware is any physical device that interacts with software. For example, your computer itself is hardware, as are your keyboard, your mouse, and even your screen.

Hardware is a mechanical device that interacts with software. Adobe Photoshop, Microsoft Word, and even your Scratch projects are examples of software. They interact with your computer, which is hardware.

Some brilliant people have invented other types of hardware devices that connect to your computer and that you can use to control Scratch programs. One such device is called the Makey Makey.

A Makey Makey plugs into a USB port on your computer and then you can use it to simulate key presses and mouse clicks by connecting wires to different real-world objects.

Figure 11-11 shows a Makey Makey being used to create a keyboard from alphabet soup letters.

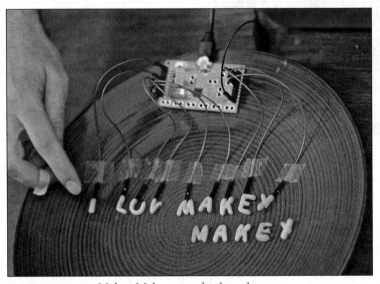

FIGURE 11-11 Makey Makey soup keyboard
Photo courtesy of JoyLabz, LLC

Makey Makey was created by JoyLabz, LLC and can be purchased from http://makeymakey.com/.

Using a Makey Makey, you can program a piano in Scratch (using the blocks you learned about in Adventure 10) and then use objects such as bananas as keys! You can connect wires to pieces of tinfoil on the floor that play drums in a Scratch project when you step on them. Or you can hold one wire and give another wire to your friend and make actions happen in Scratch when you and your friend high five! There are so many things you can do with a Makey Makey!

To understand how the Makey Makey works and what you can do with it, you first need to know a little bit about electricity.

Understanding Electricity

Electricity makes our world of computers and the web go round. But, what is it?

Electricity is a form of energy that can build up in one place or that can flow between two places. When it builds up in one place, it's called static electricity. This is the electricity that builds up when you shuffle across a carpet or pet your cat.

Static electricity is when electricity doesn't move and gets built up.

When electricity moves from one place to another, it's called current electricity, or an electric current. This is the type of electricity that powers your computer, your phone, electric lights, toasters, and much more.

Electric current is when electricity moves from one place to another.

Lightning is a very large electric current, but it can help you understand how the much smaller electric current that Makey Makey uses works.

Lightning builds up in one place (in the clouds) and then turns into current electricity by moving from one storm cloud to a storm cloud with less stored electricity, or from a storm cloud to the earth. In order to move from one place to another, the electricity needs to have something to move through. For example, lightning moves through the air. The path that an electric current flows over is called a conductor.

DEFINITIONS

A **conductor** is a channel that electricity can travel through.

The clouds, air, and earth form a path, or loop, called an electric circuit. Without one of these three parts, there would be no lightning.

Hardware, like your computer or the Makey Makey, uses electric circuits made up of a place with a positive charge, a place with a negative charge, and a conductor that is typically made of metal wire. When current is flowing through the circuit, the electronic device can work. When it's not flowing, the electronic device can't work.

Understanding Makey Makey

Makey Makey lets you create circuits using wires and other conductors to control your computer. Take a look at the close-up of Makey Makey shown in Figure 11-12. It has numerous spots where you can connect wires, and a row of spots on the bottom that are labeled "earth." Just like lightning, when electricity flows from one of the points in the upper part of the Makey Makey to any one of the spots labeled "earth," a circuit is formed.

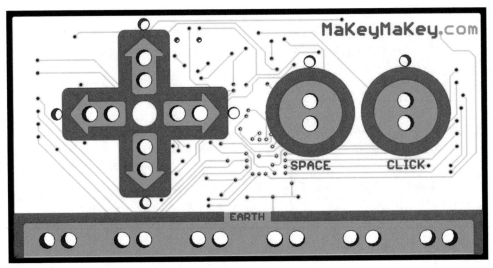

FIGURE 11-12 Makey Makey

The circuits that Makey Makey forms send signals to your computer that make it think that a keyboard key was pressed or the mouse button was clicked. You can then write programs in Scratch to detect those events!

The fun part about Makey Makey is that you can use different types of conductors (in addition to the wires) to form the circuits. For example, in Figure 11-13, bananas are being used as conductors. When you hold a wire connected to an "earth" terminal and touch a banana connected to one of the other terminals on Makey Makey, you complete the circuit and a signal is sent to your computer.

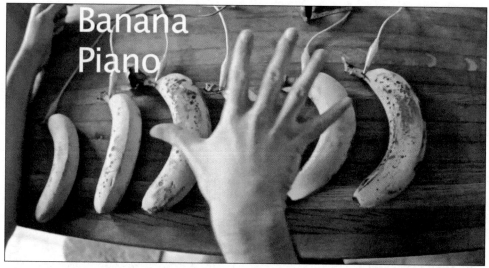

FIGURE 11-13 A banana keyboard

The next section explains conductivity and what types of things can be used as conductors.

Understanding Conductivity

A conductor is anything that electricity can flow through.

Different materials have different abilities to conduct electricity. For example, metals are great conductors, which is why they're used to make wire. Air is a poor conductor, but it can conduct electricity when the electric charge is large enough (as in the case of lightning).

Metal isn't the only material that can conduct electricity easily, however. Water also can conduct electricity. Pencil lead, which is made from graphite, is also able to conduct electricity. Plastic, rubber, ordinary rocks, and wood are all examples of materials that can't conduct electricity.

Because water is a conductor and your body contains a large percentage of water, you can act as a conductor! Other things that can act as conductors include

- Fruits and vegetables
- Tin foil
- Any metal object
- Wet dirt
- A glass of juice
- Pretty much anything that's wet

Examples of things that make poor conductors include

- Clothing
- Glass
- Non-metal furniture
- Walls
- Air

CHALLENGE

Look around you. Can you identify which objects would make good conductors and which would make poor conductors?

Large electric currents, such as lightning or electrical outlets in your home, can be dangerous and are nothing to play around with. The electric current that Makey Makey uses is very small, however, and is thus completely safe.

To watch Eva and Chris experiment with the Makey Makey, visit the companion website at `www.wiley.com/go/adventuresincoding` and choose Adventure 11!

Sensing with the PicoBoard

Another device that you can connect to your computer to control Scratch programs is the PicoBoard, shown in Figure 11-14.

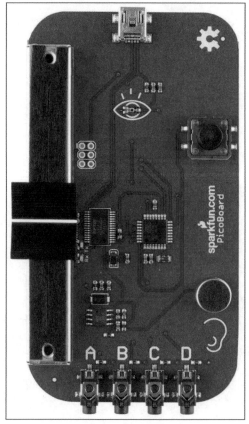

FIGURE 11-14 The PicoBoard
Photo courtesy of SparkFun Electronics

The Pico Board was created by SparkFun Electronics and can be purchased at `https://www.sparkfun.com/products/11888`.

The PicoBoard has several sensors on it that you can use with special PicoBoard Scratch blocks to control your Scratch programs and get information from the outside world into your projects.

To use the special PicoBoard blocks, click Add an Extension in the More Blocks Block Palette. Inside the Add an Extension pop-up window, you see some extensions, including the PicoBoard extension, as shown in Figure 11-15.

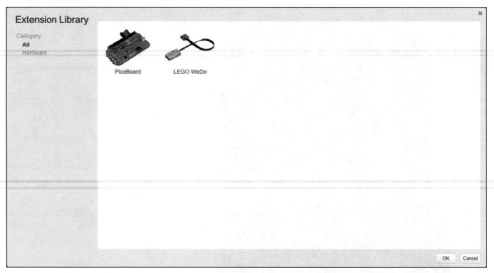

FIGURE 11-15 Adding the PicoBoard extension

After you add the Extension Library, you'll see the new PicoBoard blocks in your More Blocks Block Palette, and some instructions will appear for installing the PicoBoard browser extension so that you can use it with Scratch.

If you have a PicoBoard, you can then detect changes to the sound and light sensor, or when the button on PicoBoard is pressed or its slider is slid.

By connecting your computer to other hardware such as a Makey Makey or a PicoBoard, the world of interactive programs comes alive!

Further Adventures in Coding

Achievement Unlocked: **Scratch Community**

To view examples of other Scratch projects that use the Makey Makey and PicoBoard visit the following links:

- Makey Makey Scratch projects: `https://scratch.mit.edu/studios/230629/`

- PicoBoard projects: `https://scratch.mit.edu/studios/94856/`

Appendix A

Installing the Scratch Offline Editor

THERE ARE TIMES when you want to create projects using Scratch, but you don't have an Internet connection. Have no fear! That's where Scratch's Offline Editor comes in. With Scratch's Offline Editor, you can create and continue working on your projects even without a connection to the Internet. In this appendix, you learn how to install the Scratch Offline Editor on your computer.

Installing the Scratch Offline Editor on Windows

To install the Scratch Offline Editor to your Windows computer, use the following steps.

The first step is to download and install Adobe AIR.

1. Go to the download page at `https://scratch.mit.edu/scratch2 download/`, as shown in Figure A-1.

2. If you don't already have Adobe AIR installed, click the Download link next to the Windows title, as shown in Figure A-2.

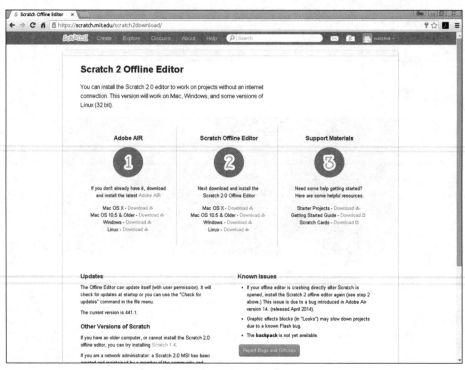

FIGURE A-1 The Scratch Offline Editor download page

FIGURE A-2 Step 1 to download Adobe AIR

If you are unsure which download is appropriate for you, simply click the link that reads Adobe AIR above the download options; this will automatically detect what version of the download you need.

3. On the Adobe download page, click Download Now, as shown in Figure A-3.

FIGURE A-3 Downloading Adobe AIR

4. After your download has completed, navigate to your Downloads folder and locate the `AdobeAIRInstaller` file. Double-click to open it. The Program Manager opens.

5. Click Run to give your computer permission to run this file, as shown in Figure A-4.

FIGURE A-4 Running the Adobe AIR installer

6. The Adobe AIR program manager box opens to alert you that the file has completed installation, as shown in Figure A-5.

FIGURE A-5 Installation of Adobe AIR is complete

7. Click Finish.

You've now installed Adobe AIR on your Windows machine. Navigate back to the Scratch Offline Editor download page at `https://scratch.mit.edu/scratch2download` to download the Scratch Offline Editor.

1. Click the Windows download link for your Windows operating system, as shown in Figure A-6.

FIGURE A-6 Downloading the Scratch Offline Editor

2. The file downloads to your Downloads folder.

3. Go to your Downloads folder and double-click the file to open it.

4. A security dialog box asks you if you would like to Run or Cancel the file, as shown in Figure A-7. Click Run.

FIGURE A-7 Running the Scratch Offline Editor installer

5. You see an installation box that offers you options, such as the ability to create a shortcut to Scratch from your desktop, as shown in Figure A-8. Check the boxes to set your preferences and click Continue.

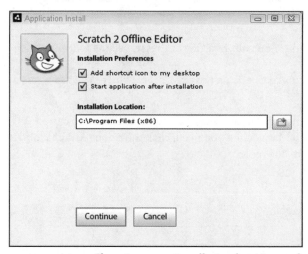

FIGURE A-8 Choosing your installation location and preferences

An installation progress bar lets you know how the installation is coming along, as shown in Figure A-9.

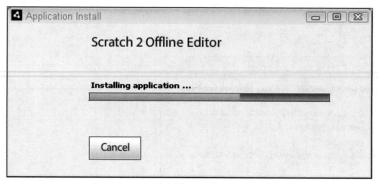

FIGURE A-9 Installing the Offline Editor

6. After it has completed installation, the Scratch Offline Editor has been installed on your computer! If you selected the option to create a shortcut, you should see the Scratch the Cat logo shortcut right on your desktop.

Now you can program using Scratch from whatever location you like, regardless of whether you have an Internet connection.

Installing the Scratch Offline Editor to Your Mac Operating System

To install the Scratch Offline Editor on your MacOS computer, use the following steps.

1. Go to `https://scratch.mit.edu/scratch2download/`. You see a screen similar to Figure A-10.

2. Install Adobe AIR. Click the appropriate Mac OS Download link (see Figure A-11). If you are unsure of which Mac version you need, click the Adobe AIR link, and it will detect the appropriate download.

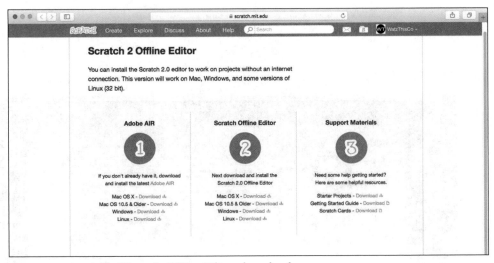

FIGURE A-10 The Scratch Offline Editor download page

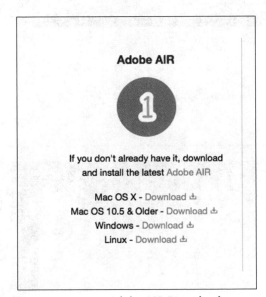

FIGURE A-11 Adobe AIR Download

3. You see the Adobe AIR Download screen, as shown in Figure A-12. Click the Download Now button in the lower-right corner.

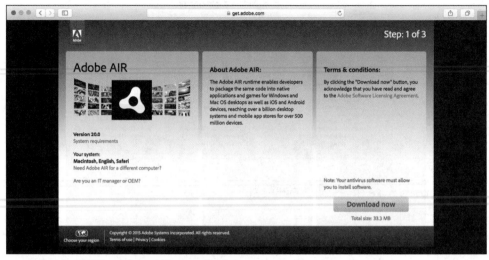

FIGURE A-12 The Adobe AIR download screen

4. Once your download has started, click Next, as shown in Figure A-13.

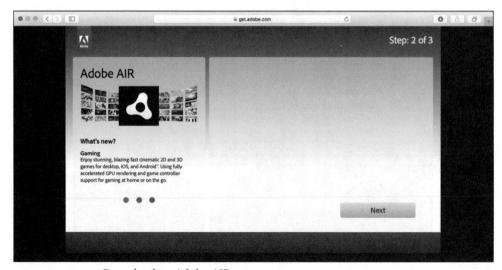

FIGURE A-13 Downloading Adobe AIR

This completes the installation of Adobe AIR on your MacOS computer. Navigate back to scratch.mit.edu/scratch2download/ to download and install the Scratch Offline Editor.

1. Click the Download link next to the appropriate Mac operating system version (see Figure A-14) and your download will begin.

FIGURE A-14 Step 2 of downloading the Scratch Offline Editor

2. Once your file has finished downloading, locate the Install Scratch 2.app file in your Downloads folder (see Figure A-15) and click it.

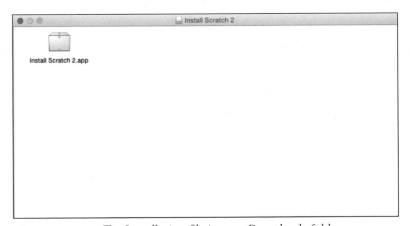

FIGURE A-15 The Installation file in your Downloads folder

By default, Mac OS only allows you to install programs from the Mac App Store. If your security preferences are set this way, you may see the notification shown in Figure A-16.

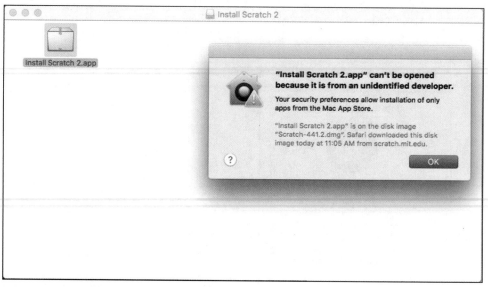

FIGURE A-16 The Mac security preferences

To adjust the preferences and allow your computer to install the Scratch Offline Editor, use the following steps.

1. Click the Apple icon in the upper-left corner of your computer screen.

2. Choose System Preferences, as shown in Figure A-17.

FIGURE A-17 Choosing System Preferences

3. In the first column, choose Security & Privacy.

Your Security and Privacy Preferences window opens. You may need to click the lock and type your password to make changes. In this window, you have the options of allowing downloads from anywhere, or just allowing the Scratch Installer to open anyway.

4. Click Open Anyway.

Scratch Offline Editor now opens. You may see a pop-up window like the one in Figure A-18. If so, click Open.

FIGURE A-18 Your computer is checking the security of the file

Scratch begins downloading, with a progress bar, as shown in Figure A-19.

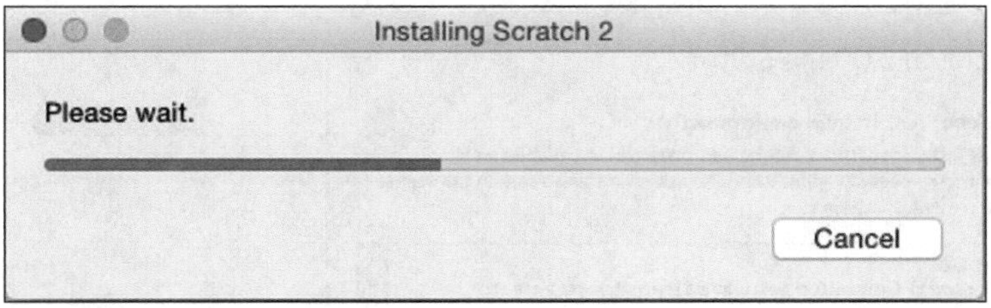

FIGURE A-19 Scratch is being installed

When the installation is complete, locate the Scratch Installer in your dock at the bottom of your screen. Click the icon and a window with your Offline Editor preferences opens, as shown in Figure A-20. Choose your preference in the window.

FIGURE A-20 The Scratch Offline Editor Preferences

After you've chosen your preferences, click Continue.

The Terms and Conditions window opens. After reading the terms and conditions (see Figure A-21), click the I Agree button. You may need to enter your password to allow Adobe AIR to complete its installation.

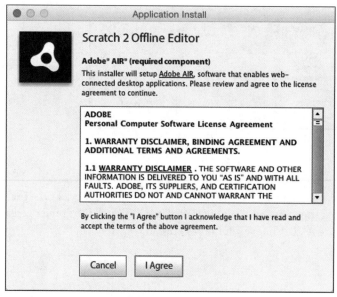

FIGURE A-21 The Adobe Air Scratch Offline Editor Terms and Conditions

Your Offline Editor completes its installation, as shown in Figure A-22.

FIGURE A-22 The Scratch Offline Editor is completing installation

When your file has completed downloading, open your Applications folder and locate the `Scratch 2.app` file. Drag it to your dock, as shown in Figure A-23.

FIGURE A-23 The Scratch Offline Editor in your dock

You now have the Scratch Offline Editor installed on your computer, with easy access from your dock. You can now create your Scratch programs wherever you are!

Other Resources

Other resources are available at `https://scratch.mit.edu/scratch2down loads/`. From Step 3 on this page, you can access links to a Getting Started guide, along with a link to a downloadable folder containing a wide range of starter projects. You can download these and work with them in your Scratch Offline Editor any time you like! There is also a link to download printable Scratch Cards, for on-the-go reference. The cards contain simple instructions for common codes that you can try out and use in your programs.

Appendix B
Testing Your Programs

TESTING IS A vital part of programming. It's said that you should spend as much time testing your programs as you spend writing them. In this appendix, we show you ten simple techniques, tools, and tips for finding and preventing errors, or **bugs**, in your programs.

In programming, anything that causes your program to run incorrectly, or not at all, is called a **bug**.

Practice Proper Planning

The key to success in programming is planning. If your program is going to involve multiple scenes, scripts, or sprites, sketch it out on paper or in a drawing program before you start coding.

Another name for this rough drawing of your program is **wireframe**. For example, Figure B-1 shows how you might draw a wireframe for the 3-Ring Circus program that you created in Adventure 5.

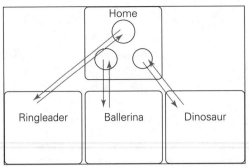

FIGURE B-1 A wireframe for the 3-Ring Circus program

DEFINITIONS

A **wireframe** is a visual sketch of a program.

When you're drawing a wireframe, don't worry about how it looks or about getting everything perfect. The idea is just to create something visual that you can look at while you're programming to help you see how all the parts fit together.

Ask Other People to Test

Want to know the secret that every great coder uses to make their programs as good as they can be? It's quite simple, actually: They have other programmers look at their work, and just as importantly, they have non-programmers test out their programs regularly. Having another set of eyes (or many more) look at your program will often help you discover the source of bugs or potential problems. Even better, your testers will often come up with ideas for improving your program that you didn't think of! And, we all want our programs to be as good as they can be, right?

A big part of testing is a process called *debugging*. Debugging is the process of figuring out why a program isn't working as expected and fixing it.

CHRIS & EVA SAY

The name "debugging" was made popular by Grace Hopper, a computer programmer who invented many of the technologies that led to the invention of Scratch and every other computer programming language we use today. When she was programming in the 1940s, she actually fixed a problem with a computer by removing a moth from it.

Look for Possible Invalid Input

Do you have a sprite that asks for the user's age? What happens if people type a word into that input? Does your program ask them to try again with a number, or does the program break? Testing any type of user input for invalid entries and providing the users with good feedback when they enter something unexpected makes programs run smoother and leads to happier users.

Figure B-2 shows a bit of a program that could cause problems if someone enters letters instead of the expected number, or enters a number that's not a valid age.

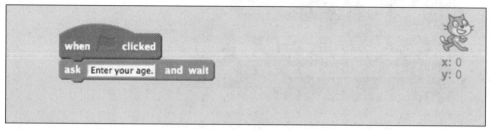

FIGURE B-2 A program that might cause problems

To make sure that the users only provide a number greater than 0 and less than 120, you can use operator blocks. Specifically, you use the `if () then` and `repeat until ()` blocks, as shown in Figure B-3.

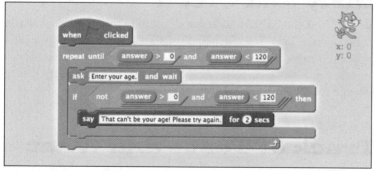

FIGURE B-3 Adding blocks to test input values

Use Comments Often

Comments that describe your code are helpful for when you want to change or add to your program. They're also a great way to track down bugs in your programs.

For example, in the program shown in Figure B-4, we've used comments to explain what the most important blocks do.

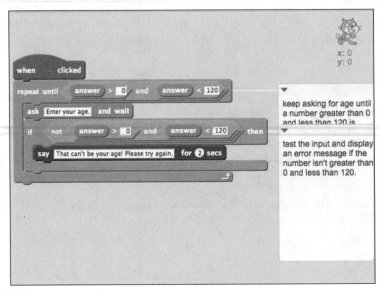

FIGURE B-4 Using comments to help with debugging

Test Early and Often

When should you test? You should start testing your projects shortly after you start coding them — if not sooner! The best time to find and fix a bug is right after it makes its way into your code. Likewise, if you run and track tests after any significant change to a program happens, you'll have a complete record of your tests and can use that to quickly track down and fix new problems.

Keep Track of Tests and What Breaks Things

One of the most important things you can do as a new programmer is keep a notebook, or a text file on your computer, that tracks what you did and how you did it. You should also track tests that you perform and bugs that you find and fix.

Tracking your testing makes it much easier to fix things that go wrong in the future. Keeping track of tests can be as simple as writing down every time you test your program, what went wrong when you tested it, and how you fixed it.

Use Custom Blocks

When you're writing complex programs, you'll often find that certain functionality takes a large number of blocks to build. Having a large number of blocks linked together in the Scripts Area can make your program difficult to manage and test.

To reduce the complexity of your programs, look for opportunities to create custom blocks. After you've created a custom block, you can use that block as a stand-in for sections of code and make your sprite's Scripts Area look much cleaner.

You can even move the code that declares the custom block off of the visible part of the Scripts Area, so that it doesn't clutter up your screen.

Use Sliders for Numbers

When you ask users to enter a number, you can easily prevent them from entering letters or invalid numbers by using a slider. Sliders are one of the ways to display variables on the Stage.

To change a variable to display on the Stage as a slider, right-click it and select Slider. The variable display on the Stage changes to a slider, as shown in Figure B-5.

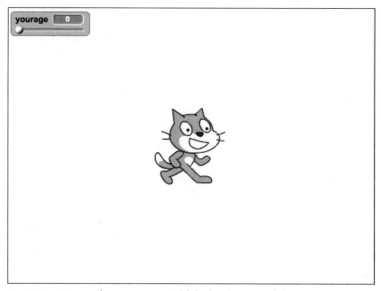

FIGURE B-5 Changing a variable's display to a slider

By default, sliders have a minimum value of 0 and a maximum value of 100. You can change this by right-clicking the slider and selecting Set Min and Max. You see a pop-up window, as shown in Figure B-6, where you can enter new minimum and maximum values.

FIGURE B-6 Setting minimum and maximum values

Keep Learning

This book is just the tip of the iceberg in the vast ocean of available knowledge about Scratch and about coding in general. There's always more to learn, and there will always be people, videos, websites, and books that are more than happy to help you learn it. As you continue learning, you'll find new ways to build better programs, and in return, create programs with fewer bugs.

Some of our favorite resources for learning about Scratch are the following:

- Scratch Wiki at `http://wiki.scratch.mit.edu/wiki/Scratch_Wiki`: The Scratch Wiki is a giant source of information and tutorials about Scratch. The articles here are all written by members of the Scratch community, and the site is supported by the Scratch team. With around 1,000 articles available on the Scratch Wiki, it will be a good long time before you run out of things to learn there!

- Scratch video tutorials at `https://scratch.mit.edu/help/videos/`: The Scratch video tutorials are a great way to learn more about coding with Scratch by watching someone else use it. The videos start with an introduction to Scratch and then progress through a series of tutorials and some videos about the Paint Editor.

To learn about coding beyond Scratch, we recommend the following resources:

- *JavaScript For Kids For Dummies* (Wiley, 2015), by Chris Minnick and Eva Holland: JavaScript is the most popular and widely used programming language in the world. If you want to take the next step in your coding adventure, this book will show you how to create fun games, interactive stories, and much more using JavaScript.

- Code.org at `https://code.org`: Code.org contains projects designed to teach kids how to program. You can learn to build a *Minecraft* adventure, a *Star Wars* game, and more!

Keep Practicing

One of the most important things you can do to become really good at Scratch, or anything else for that matter, is to practice it. You've probably heard it all before, but practicing is truly the best way to master something—be it a computer programming language or making sandwiches. The key is practice. When you repeatedly perform an activity, that activity becomes a normal or usual part of your life. Become very familiar with a topic by practicing it, and it will become second nature!

A good tip to becoming a master Scratcher is to schedule a specific time to practice coding and stick to that time. Learning new things can sometimes be hard, especially when you're learning a new language. It's best to try not to get too frustrated when you're practicing coding, and to take deep breaths if you can't figure something out.

If you are finding that you just can't figure out where the bug is in your program, it's important to take a break from it. Very often, the answer is right in front of you, but you can't see it because you've been looking at the program for too long and you've become kind of blind to it.

If you find yourself becoming frustrated or annoyed during your practice, stand up, take a deep breath, and have a good long stretch. Then maybe do a couple of jumping jacks to get all your blood moving. Take a break from your code. When you return, you may find the answer sitting there waiting for you!

Best of luck in your Scratch practice!

Glossary

application A set of programming commands that follow each other in a particular order to accomplish tasks. *Application* is another name for a computer program.

argument Any value that is sent into a program or a custom block.

array A variable that can hold multiple values using the same name.

backdrop What displays behind your sprites on the Stage. A costume for the Stage sprite.

block A puzzle-piece shape in Scratch that is used to create commands.

Boolean block A hexagonally shaped Scratch block that stands for a true or false value.

branching Programming commands that choose between multiple paths.

broadcasting In Scratch, a broadcast sends a secret message that only sprites can tune into and hear.

bug Anything that causes your program to run incorrectly or not at all.

cap block A Scratch block that is used to stop a script or project.

C-block A C-block is a Scratch block that stack blocks can fit into. They perform loops or make decisions.

chat bot A program that talks, or chats, with people.

coding A common name for computer programming. When you code, you're using a computer language to tell computers what to do.

command An instruction, written in a programming language, that tells a computer to do a task.

comment A note that you leave in a program that's intended to be read by people rather than computers.

conductor A channel that electricity can travel through.

curator A manager or guardian in charge of the selections displayed in a Scratch Studio.

custom blocks Single blocks that represent a group of blocks or a script.

electric current When electricity moves from one place to another.

event Something that happens in a program and that triggers an action.

focus When you click an item in a browser to highlight it or make it active, you are giving that item focus.

font Also known as typefaces. The design of a complete set of letters and numbers.

hardware A mechanical device that interacts with software.

hat block A Scratch block that triggers the start of a script.

loop A block that causes the commands contained within it to repeat one or more times.

metadata Information used to describe a program. It can contain information such as the creator of the project, the tags associated with your project, or instructions on how to use your program. Metadata is not part of your code, but rather describes the details of your project.

nesting When a programming command, or a Scratch block, is contained within another command or Scratch block. For example, the commands within a loop are nested within the loop.

operations Specific tasks that work with values to produce results.

persistent Data that remains part of a program after the program stops running. Scratch variables are persistent.

pixel One of the many tiny dots that make up images on a computer screen.

pixelated The look of an image that has been enlarged to the point where you can see the individual pixels that make up the image.

programmer A person who writes computer programs.

programming language A language used for giving instructions to computers.

remixing The process of creating a different version of something.

reporter block An oval-shaped Scratch block that contains a value.

Scratch A programming language designed for beginners that was invented at the Massachusetts Institute of Technology (MIT).

script A computer program that is smaller or has a more limited purpose than an *application*.

sprite A character, or actor, in a Scratch program.

stack block A Scratch block that represents an action that does something within your program.

stage The area in the Scratch Project Editor where sprites act out scripts that you write.

static electricity Electricity that doesn't move.

submit input The process of sending the words or numbers typed into a form to a program.

variable A box that you can give a name to and store data inside of.

waveform The visual representation of a sound.

wireframe A visual sketch of a program.

Index